Most Camino books talk about life in
advice on what to see or what to do. Some
and myths. Others are spiritual or religiou:
but . . . I can tell you that if you cross the threshold of this book,
you will get to know the Camino itself. By walking *My Own Pace*
(and I mean walking, not reading), Bryan will take you to the heart
of the Camino: The People. Multi-faceted people full of faces,
angles, and edges. Just people with all the complications of simple
people. And Bryan shows himself to these people as he is: with his
limitations and fears, and with his immense courage and humble
heart. He lays bare his weaknesses and lets us follow the journey in
which his heart and his "flawed DNA" led him to many lessons.

But what I discover most, as I enjoy this wonderful book,
is how many lives Bryan changed because of his "own pace."
So, I must warn you, intrepid traveler, beware if you begin this
adventure because it is very possible that if you dare to walk with
Bryan, you will end up, at the very least, getting to know yourself
better, and dare I say it . . . it is very possible that this story will
change your heart as it has changed mine.

Jose Mari Ardanaz, founder of El Camino People

[*My Own Pace*] is a magic account of a magical journey. Bryan
sums up perfectly the atmosphere, spirit, and compassion of the
ancient pilgrimage of el Camino de Santiago. It's not just a book
for pilgrims, it's a book for all of us who need to know how to
overcome our challenges, how to be a better person, and how we
can take that better 'you' home to those you love.

Dan Mullins, host of *My Camino–The Podcast*

Bryan's story of walking the Camino de Santiago is familiar to
me as a pilgrim, yet offers a completely new perspective that made
me appreciate more richly his Camino experience as well as my
own. His empowering tale of overcoming hardship makes this a
must-read for those facing their own obstacles. Buen Camino!

Kevin Donahue, host of *Sacred Steps Podcast*

i

My Own Pace

A Story of
Strength and Adversity
on the
Camino de Santiago

Bryan Paul Steward

WYNNEWOOD PUBLISHING

Wynnewood Publishing, Burlington, New Jersey

Cover design by Dalton Ackerman

Some names and identifying details have been changed to
protect the privacy of individuals.

Disclaimer: The content of this book is for informational
purposes only and is not intended to be a guidebook for
hiking the Camino.

ISBN 978-0-578-35996-0 (paperback)

Library of Congress Control Number: 2022901609

Printed in the United States of America.

For Madeline

EL CAMINO DE SANTIAGO

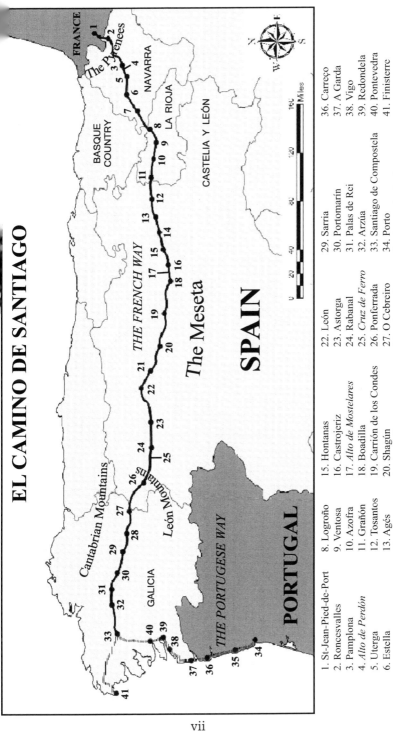

1. St-Jean-Pied-de-Port
2. Roncesvalles
3. Pamplona
4. *Alto de Perdón*
5. Uterga
6. Estella
7. Los Arcos
8. Logroño
9. Ventosa
10. Azofra
11. Grañón
12. Tosantos
13. Agés
14. Burgos
15. Hontanas
16. Castrojeriz
17. *Alto de Mostelares*
18. Boadilla
19. Carrión de los Condes
20. Shagún
21. Mansilla
22. León
23. Astorga
24. Rabanal
25. *Cruz de Ferro*
26. Ponferrada
27. O Cebreiro
28. Triacastela
29. Sarria
30. Portomarín
31. Palas de Rei
32. Arzúa
33. Santiago de Compostela
34. Porto
35. Povoa de Varzim
36. Carreço
37. A Garda
38. Vigo
39. Redondela
40. Pontevedra
41. Finisterre

CONTENTS

FOREWORD
BY PATRICK GRAY AND
JUSTIN SKEESUCK

Every life has challenges. Some obstacles come without warning, there are those you see coming and can't avoid, and then there are others you create for yourself. Regardless of where your struggles come from, you are the only one who can face and overcome them—because they are yours and yours alone. But so many think that "because a struggle is mine, I must face it alone."

And we listen to the lies that limit us . . .

I'm not enough.

I have no place in this world.

Someone will do better.

I'm not worthy of help.

I am a burden.

No matter what challenge your journey of life presents you, no one can walk your path better than you can—as long as you accept that you are enough and that you have an important place in this world.

My Own Pace

When you embrace these two truths, you will begin to realize you are worthy of the help you receive, and you are a burden to no one.

Though the struggles you face are yours, they are never meant to be faced alone. Every step you take, every decision, every relationship is only possible because you are there in that moment facing whatever it is you are facing, making the decisions you deem best, walking with whomever you choose. The most important thing you can do as you navigate life is let other people into your story so you don't face life's struggles alone.

While no one can walk your path for you, they can walk it with you.

So crack open the pages of this book and embrace the beauty of letting others walk by your side—just make sure you walk at your own pace.

Patrick Gray and **Justin Skeesuck**, authors of *I'll Push You*

1

FIRST STEPS

From August through October 2017, I walked five hundred miles from St-Jean-Pied-de-Port, France to Santiago de Compostela, Spain, on the trail known as the Camino de Santiago. What made my journey unique was the added challenge of having the neuromuscular disease called Becker muscular dystrophy. When I decided to hike the Camino, I was twenty-four years old, a year out of college, working part-time, and struggling to place myself into the next part of my life. The story of this journey began well before the Camino or muscular dystrophy were even thoughts in my mind.

Growing up, my family constantly traveled around the United States during the summer, usually involving hiking, camping, and long road trips. At three years old, during a hiking trip in New England, I complained of weakness in my legs that I described as my "knees hurting." The initial thought was that I had contracted Lyme disease from a tick bite. Lyme disease was rapidly spreading across the Northeast and relatively little was known about all its symptoms. This seemed a likely possibility, but a blood test produced negative results. After the relief of learning that I did not have Lyme disease, my doctor and parents were still puzzled about my weakness. I continued to complain and ask to be carried up stairs and hills. Preschool teachers noticed I had trouble running, jumping, and hopping, and I fell frequently. My pediatrician continued

My Own Pace

to downplay concerns, saying, "He will probably always be a little clumsy."

As I grew older, my muscle weakness worsened. I suffered from leg cramps and tightness that caused me to walk on my toes. School gym teachers and classmates often teased me, and my parents tried to correct my walk. At age seven, I distinctly remember my father's frustration during a vacation in Watkins Glen, New York. I complained about walking up a hill and wanted to be carried. He snapped at me, "All the places we go on vacation require a lot of walking. You need to get used to it and stop complaining."

The arguments about hiking increased as I grew too old to be carried. All of this changed at eight years old, after my mother received a phone call from her sister. My aunt's son had just been diagnosed with Becker muscular dystrophy after suffering from weakness similar to my own. When my mother learned this condition is genetic, her first thought was, "Bryan has it too!"

Becker muscular dystrophy is a neuromuscular disease that causes progressive deterioration of the skeletal and cardiac muscles, ultimately robbing one of the ability to walk. There is no cure for muscular dystrophy, although several drugs exist that can prolong the quality of life. Becker muscular dystrophy, like the similar but more severe Duchenne muscular dystrophy, is an X-linked genetic defect, meaning the condition is passed on from mother to son. Women are generally unaffected by this condition but can be carriers. My grandmother was unknowingly a carrier, so my mother and her two sisters also became unexpected carriers.

With the diagnosis came yearly visits to a neurologist to monitor changes in strength and most importantly, my heart and respiratory muscles. I dreaded being poked and prodded for hours, including ultrasounds, x-rays, and other tests that seemed so unnecessary. Although I disliked these visits, the neurologist was a caring and knowledgeable doctor who took a special interest in my case and always gave us hope for a mild outcome.

The prognosis of Becker muscular dystrophy, more than other forms of muscular dystrophy, varies greatly. My neurologist summarized the variance perfectly when he said, "I have patients who are in a wheelchair at ten and others who use a cane at sixty." I appeared to be on a less aggressive path.

As I moved into my teenage years, I grew stronger and built muscle mass but struggled to run, walk up stairs, and lift heavy objects. Children in school still teased me for my weakness and inability to keep up with them. During my last visit with my pediatric neurologist, shortly before my eighteenth birthday, he asked if I was having more trouble walking long distances or up steps. I said no, but the answer in my mind was very different. He looked unconvinced and went on to explain how I would soon begin to have more problems.

During college, I noticed changes in my strength. Walking up steps became more difficult, and people in public would often ask me if I was hurt. Finding elevators and places without steps became a common occurrence for me when other people were around. Being seen as weak scared me. Despite being faced with the reality that my condition was progressing, suddenly I chose to hike, go on long walks, and do tasks that required strength. As inspirational as this would seem at face value, these changes stemmed from denial. I thought that maybe if I pushed myself to the limits, then I could pretend muscular dystrophy had no impact on me. I wanted to believe the lie I told my doctor was true.

My college years were some of the most active of my life. I spent the summer of 2013 living and working at a dude ranch in Wyoming and the following two summers on solo trips around the American West. The more I did, the more muscular dystrophy felt like something I could ignore, but in reality I was being haunted by a daunting specter. Facing these challenges was my way of resisting reality.

My Own Pace

While attending The College of New Jersey, I became involved with a group called the Society for Treatment and Awareness of Neuromuscular Disease (S.T.A.N.D.). The club president, living with Duchenne muscular dystrophy, welcomed me into the organization. Initially I dreaded going to the meetings and talking about subjects I did not want to have any association with, but I continued to participate and hoped it would lead somewhere good. Part of me wanted to let go of the fear I felt towards my condition and embrace who I was. I quickly became a leading member and eventually president myself.

Our group organized several fundraisers and events on campus, including a walk across New Jersey. A close friend of mine agreed to walk with me on the three-day, forty-eight mile journey from the Delaware River to the Atlantic Ocean. The walk amounted to little more than an article in a newspaper, but this event had a strong impact on me. When we reached the warm water of the Atlantic Ocean, I felt that anything I set my mind on was possible. Maybe this adventurous spirit was born from a refusal to accept the truth, but I wanted to keep pushing my bounds. My immediate thought was to plan a walk across the entire United States after graduating college, but that never happened.

After several failed post-college interviews for full-time jobs, I became stuck in a series of temp jobs that went nowhere. I decided to make the most of this lull in my life and finally plan a big adventure. Maintaining my current job would not be possible if I took off a year to walk across the United States, but I remembered hearing about a hike in Spain that was around five hundred miles long, the Camino de Santiago.

The Camino de Santiago is a network of interconnected roads and trails across Europe leading to the tomb of Saint James in the city of Santiago de Compostela, Spain. In the Catholic Church, walking the Camino has been considered a religious pilgrimage for over a thousand years. At the end of the journey, pilgrims are issued a certificate known as a "Compostela," certifying that one has walked at least one hundred kilometers (sixty-two miles) to Santiago. The most popular route, known as the French Way, begins at the northern foot of the Pyrenees Mountains in southern France and spans five hundred miles, passing through cities, villages, farmland, forests, and mountains. In modern times, the pilgrimage is more recreational than religious but still maintains a spiritual connection to healing, growth, and self-reflection.

To my amazement, my boss granted me seven weeks off to attempt the hike. My request for time off from work came four months before I was to begin my hike in August. I planned to complete the French Way of the Camino in forty days, which averaged about twelve miles a day, excluding rest days. This journey would not be like walking across New Jersey. I needed to climb over the Pyrenees Mountains, hike through the flat desolate region of Spain known as the Meseta, and then cross a series of mountains in Galicia, before arriving in Santiago. I had no idea what to expect. My only thoughts were to take it slow and not injure myself as I trained over the coming months. Most people were concerned about my well-being and questioned my decision to hike the Camino. I knew they were probably right. Intense physical exertion is not recommended for people with muscular dystrophy, so I needed to be careful not to push myself too hard.

Every day I walked at parks and trails near my home and slowly increased my distance from five to sixteen miles. I fell a lot and wondered if my body could handle what the Camino would throw at me. As the days went on, I began to feel stronger. Walking became a part-time job. Friends would occasionally join me, but I walked mostly alone. By the end of July, I had walked over four hundred miles, and I felt great. I knew I was capable of going the distance, but I would be lying if I said I was not scared. During the past few years, my adventures were a way of dodging reality, but the Camino might actually be the place where I could no longer hide. How sore and tired could I become before I gave up? I was about to find out.

Over the coming weeks, I found myself learning and reflecting as I faced fears and weaknesses that challenged me in ways I never imagined.

2

BUEN CAMINO

After nearly forty-eight hours of connecting flights from Philadelphia to Paris, and a long train ride across the French countryside, I arrived in St-Jean-Pied-de-Port around 10:30 p.m. on August 17. As I stepped off the train and hoisted my red hiking backpack over my shoulders, I took a deep breath and looked around the dark, empty station. I had no firm plans beyond arriving in St-Jean, and I half expected to sleep in an alleyway. A group of a half dozen people from my train with backpacks as large as mine began walking into town, so I followed. Everyone wanted to find the Pilgrim's Office that I expected was closed at this hour.

The streetlights from the town created a welcoming feeling for my true first steps on this journey. All of my traveling from here would be on foot until Santiago. The worn cobblestone road leading up to the office was extremely steep and difficult to climb, and my feet slipped on the smooth rocks. To my delight, we found the office still open. In the brightly lit room was a long row of tables with Camino brochures and maps, and two people ready to check us in. They must have anticipated our new group of pilgrims arriving in St-Jean.

A woman sitting at one of the tables spoke English and offered to help me. Her eyes looked tired from a long day of work. I signed into a log and told her of my plans to walk five miles to Orisson the next day. She thought Orisson was booked full, and my only option would be to walk fifteen miles all the way over the Pyrenees Mountains to Ronces-valles. I explained that I had muscular dystrophy, and there was no way I could cross that section in one day.

"I'll tell you what, Orisson opens at 8:00 a.m. Come back here tomorrow morning. I will call Orisson and see if there is a bed. Sometimes people cancel reservations. Otherwise you can spend a day here in St-Jean and book a bed in Orisson for the next night. Or tomorrow you can take the alternate route around the Pyrenees to Valcarlos," she said with a hopeless look.

Taking the easy "alternate" way was not part of my plans. I wanted to see the Pyrenees, so the Napoleon Route, which it was known as, was the only option for me. I cursed myself for not thinking to reserve a bed in Orisson. The woman gave me a route map through the Pyrenees, elevation charts, and a list of hostels (known as albergues) and their contact information. I proceeded to purchase my credential book to collect stamps along the way as proof I completed the requirements of the Camino, and a white scallop shell that was the symbol of a pilgrim to wear on my pack. The woman then asked if I had a place to stay tonight, and I said no.

"Not to worry, you will stay at Anne's home," the woman said, as she directed me across the street to a house with a string of blinking lights around the white brick doorway.

I thanked the woman and ventured out onto the cobble-stone street and knocked on Anne's screen door.

"Uno momento," I heard in a raspy smoker's voice from inside and was greeted by a petite woman in her mid-sixties with long black hair and a blue dress.

Inside I was joined by an Italian couple who had been on my train. Anne told us to remove our shoes and place them on a shelf with a half dozen other pairs. Like most Americans on the Camino, placing my shoes in a communal pile was quite a foreign concept. I reluctantly complied with her wishes. This,

Buen Camino

I learned, was a common request at most albergues. The home smelled of cigarettes, and three cats lay sprawled out on the living room couch. Paintings and small knick-knacks cluttered the walls and shelves throughout the house. After I signed into the log and paid for my bed, Anne directed us upstairs to the bedrooms. I had trouble walking up the steps and nearly knocked an oil painting of the Pyrenees Mountains off the wall and readjusted it as Anne assured me it was alright.

My room for the night had eight sets of bunks crowded together. A slight breeze came in from an open screenless window. Anne introduced me to the other pilgrims who were all young and of various European nationalities. Everyone kept to themselves, writing in journals or looking over guidebooks. After lying in bed, I realized I had not eaten since Paris. There was no way I could walk tomorrow if I went nearly twenty-four hours without food, so I went back downstairs to ask Anne if there were any restaurants still open.

She directed me back down the steep road, past a church, and over a bridge to a restaurant. At night the empty streets of St-Jean seemed eerie. The surrounding buildings cast shadows that were occasionally broken by yellow streetlights. Across from the church I found a restaurant with a glow of light coming from an open door. Inside, a group of men were eating, laughing, and drinking wine. At the counter, a young boy wearing black overalls jumped off a bar stool and asked me something in French. I gave him a smile, as if to say, I was completely lost and only spoke English. He handed me a menu with everything written in French.

Again, the boy said something in French and pointed to one section of the menu, indicating that they were no longer serving meals; only food from a specific section of the menu was available. I wanted something quick, so I asked for a croissant. The boy looked at me confused. I tried to pronounce croissant in a strong French accent like an ignorant American. Still the boy looked confused and went to get his father who

9

was a chef in the kitchen. A croissant seemed like something I could surely order in France. The chef approached wearing his white food-stained apron. I repeated my request for a croissant in the best French accent I could muster, but he just frowned and put his hands up. I was thinking, "How am I in France and no one knows what a croissant is?"

Feeling the conversation was just as awkward for them as for me, they directed me down the road to another restaurant, which was the one Anne had originally recommended. The place was full of young people sitting at outside tables and drinking beer. Inside, I was thrilled to find someone at the counter who spoke English. Unfortunately, they were no longer serving food for the day. I asked if there was anything they could serve me. The chubby man behind the counter saw the desperation in my eyes and offered me a bowl of soup. Without a moment of hesitation, I agreed and was shown to a table as a setting was prepared.

Although I was in France, Spanish music played loudly throughout the restaurant, and the staff busily mopped and cleaned up for the night. The beef and vegetable soup was delicious but had large chunks of bone attached to the beef, which I was not accustomed to. I ate quickly and devoured the bread as well. As I looked around at the French and Spanish décor, cabinets filled with wine bottles, and listened to people speaking a language I did not understand, I finally felt thousands of miles away from home and completely removed from everything I was comfortable with. I was both excited and afraid of the unknown that lay before me.

The walk back up the steep road to the albergue was extremely difficult and disheartening. Getting to the top of the hill took all my strength. My legs gave out several times, and I wiped tears from my eyes. How could I cross the Pyrenees when I could barely make it up this road? I felt like the entire trip was a horrible mistake, and I had spent thousands of dollars on something I should have known was physically impossible. My excitement to be exploring somewhere on the other side of the world was quickly shedding away. I was alone.

I had trouble falling asleep that night. My thoughts were filled with anger for the decision I made to come here and concerns for what lay ahead. I felt as if I stood before a darkness with no end in sight. These fears struck at the very core of my existence, beyond the physical limitations of my body. If I failed, would I be able to look at myself the same way? How would I tell people I was too afraid to take a chance? The call of the Camino brought me here, but now I needed to summon my inner strength to take that first step the next morning and fight the refusal to muster onward. If my spirit broke now, my journey was over. I could not bear to walk away from this moment I had anticipated for so long. All I could do to prepare for the adventure was sleep. Two full days had passed since I last slept. Tomorrow's troubles could wait for tomorrow.

I was the first pilgrim awake in the morning. The room was still dark, so I used my headlamp to see while getting ready for my first official day on the Camino. The other pilgrims in the room stirred as my light cast shadows on the walls. After I went to the bathroom, filled up my water bottles, and organized the last of my gear, I went downstairs around 7:00 a.m. Just as soon as I was settled into this place, I was leaving. Thinking about how many albergues I would be staying in throughout this journey was a bit overwhelming.

My first stop of the day was to find a sporting goods store because I needed to buy a hiking pole. A good pole would help reduce the pressure of the heavy pack on my back and legs. Most pilgrims who use poles have two, but I preferred to have a free hand if I lost my balance, so I chose to use one. Since I could not find a pole to fit in my pack, and they were not allowed to be carried on the plane, I decided to wait until I arrived in Europe to buy one. I picked a retractable red one, adjusted it to my height, and made sure it felt sturdy. I still had to wait about twenty minutes for the pilgrim's office to open, so I asked a pilgrim walking by to snap a picture of me all geared up. Beyond the town, I could see the Pyrenees Mountains, slightly covered in fog, and towering over the horizon. Tomorrow I planned to be on the other side of those mountains.

I walked over to the pilgrim's office at 8:00 a.m. and was greeted by the woman I had met the day before. She remembered me and called Orisson, asking if there was a bed available, and to my amazement there was. A reservation was made for "Bryan from the United States," but it would expire at 1:00 p.m. As I headed out the door, the woman said, "Buen Camino." This Spanish greeting commonly used by pilgrims on the Camino translates to "good way" or "happy trails" in English.

My next stop was to find some breakfast and food for the trail. Most of the stores were still closed, and I did not have the time to waste. I knew the route was going to be difficult heading into the mountains, and making it to Orisson by 1:00 p.m. was a stretch. Luckily, I found a small family-owned bakery and bought a package of freshly made cookies.

With the aromas of the bakery still in my nose, I ventured down the road on a pleasant downhill walk through St-Jean. The town was filled with so much color that I missed when I arrived at night. Down the main road of town known as Rue de la Citadelle, strings of green, white, and red flags, the colors of Basque nationalism, were strung from the buildings. The province of Lower Navarre, where St-Jean was located, is the center of Basque culture in southern France. Sandwiched between the Spanish and the French, they had their own distinct language and customs. Along with the colored flags, the old brick buildings had bright red roofs and shutters.

On the route leading out of town there were cement blocks with yellow arrows marking the way to Santiago. Arrows were also painted on trees and buildings, so as long as I was observant, getting lost would be unlikely. At the edge of

Buen Camino

town, the trail immediately began to gain elevation. The only thing I could do was walk slowly and take small steps. I had not trained on steep roads, and the terrain was overwhelming. Both the armies of Napoleon and Charlemagne had once marched along this road to Roncesvalles. Thinking of them provided me with some motivation, but my legs were getting tired. As the trail moved beyond St-Jean, it changed from cobblestone to pavement, though this did not make the walk any easier. The day was humid and foggy, and I was already sweating, so I stopped to take off a sweatshirt and eat some cookies. A group of about twenty pilgrims on bikes passed by while I rested and several yelled, "Buen Camino," but I had not seen another pilgrim since I left St-Jean. I guessed that I was between the early and late starters.

As the trail leveled out with green pastures and grazing sheep on the sides of the road, I heard soft footsteps approach from behind. I turned to find a youthful looking girl of average height with a gentle smile and long golden-brown hair tucked under a purple bandana. Wearing a blue windbreaker and a black backpack with a Camino shell, I knew she was a pilgrim. She introduced herself as Beth from Norway and spoke perfect English, leading her to almost pass as an American.

Beth was nineteen and a recent high school graduate taking a gap year before starting college. She was hiking with her mother, who was a ways behind us with a Spanish woman they met the night before in St-Jean. Beth's mother had hiked portions of the Camino five different times, but this was her first time attempting to hike the entire route in one thru-hike. Their group would also be staying in Orisson tonight.

I told Beth that I had muscular dystrophy, explaining why I walked slowly on hills. She did not mind my pace, and said she saw me alone and thought I needed someone to walk with. One of my worries was that I would not find people willing to walk at my speed. Everyone says, "The Camino provides," and that appeared to be holding true. After walking with Beth

13

for a few minutes, I gained a sense that meeting new people was a purpose for her Camino, and she would not be just a passing pilgrim. We stopped to rest in a clearing of tall grass, drink some water, and wait for the others to catch up.

Beth introduced me to her mother, Alma, and the Spanish woman, Regina. Alma had long grey hair and glasses and was in her sixties. Regina was a physical education teacher in her early thirties from Madrid. She had dark blond hair beneath a blue baseball hat with sunglasses resting on the brim. With long legs, she looked as if she might break into a run at any moment and complete a marathon. She was only walking a four-day section of the Camino to Pamplona for an extended weekend.

Shortly after our rest, we approached another hill. Alma asked if I was hurt when I started slowing down. I explained that I had muscular dystrophy, but she did not understand until Beth explained it in Norwegian.

Beth and Regina went up ahead for a while as Alma and I talked with each other. She told me about her family and her previous five times walking portions of the Camino. Alma said she was happy to be walking with me because she wanted to walk slowly this time, and she explained how Beth tended to walk fast, as was evident when she first approached me alone.

After a while, we stopped to rest and eat some snacks near the hamlet of Honto, about midway to Orisson. By this time, the trail was becoming crowded as the late risers were catching up to us. The Camino in late summer and early fall is typically less busy than midsummer, but the number of pilgrims was less than I anticipated. I usually preferred to hike in solitude, but something about the Camino made company feel necessary. The idea of a pilgrimage is built around the idea of community, creating a mindset of a shared bond.

Shortly after Honto, the trail became incredibly steep, and my pace turned to a crawl. The sensation of blood pumping through my muscles made my legs tingle as my heart rate increased, and beads of sweat dripped from my forehead. Beth and Alma went ahead, and I remained with Regina. She did not speak English well but was able to express with difficulty, "You inspire me to make the Way."

Beth and Alma were waiting for us at the top of the hill before a brief flat section. The fog had lifted to reveal a beautiful view of sheep and cattle grazing along the green mountainsides. As we moved higher in elevation, the landscape became less forested. Just as quickly as the fog cleared, it rolled in again around 11:00 a.m. I kept glancing at my watch, since my window of time to make Orisson was shrinking. Alma kept reassuring me I would make it, otherwise I would have to take a taxi back to St-Jean for the night or walk to Roncesvalles, which would have been impossible for me.

As we continued, I stumbled and fell for seemingly no reason. Muscular dystrophy sometimes causes my legs to randomly give out, usually when I am tired. Everyone panicked, and Regina rushed over, picked up my pack, and helped me to my feet. I had to explain to everyone that I fall often and described myself as a "professional faller." Even though falling had become a usual occurrence in my life, the awkwardness of falling around someone was always the same. The most embarrassing scenarios were when I fell in public and a crowd of people rushed over to me. Although I rarely have a temper, these occurrences sometimes cause me to snap at people, "Stop! I'm fine!" or "Leave me alone!" This particular incident with my new Camino friends was a perfect demonstration of how I fall. I have learned not to fight gravity and go down on my knees without injury.

Shortly after my fall, the Camino led off the paved road and onto a rocky trail. Beth and Regina moved on ahead of us, and Alma continued to walk with me. More fog and clouds moved in, and it began to rain. Alma and I stopped to put our pack covers on. Continuing at a slow pace, we approached an uneven section, and Alma took my hand to keep me steady. When Alma put out her hand, I hesitated for a moment. I thought about how out of character it was of me to accept help from someone who had been a complete stranger several hours before. Thinking back to all the strangers who tried to help me when I fell, I realized there was no reason to resent their assistance. My fear of being seen as weak created a perception that these people were the cause of my weakness. Alma was teaching me to face my weakness, and this took a remarkable amount of inner strength I did not know I had.

The trail rejoined the road for the final stretch, but this was also the steepest section in the Pyrenees. Alma received a phone call from Beth that she and Regina had made it to the albergue. We were close, but it was raining harder, and my shoes were getting wet and heavy. "Just one foot in front of the other. Just one foot in front of the other," I repeated over and over in my head. My legs were becoming difficult to lift, and my steps became shorter. The trail was so steep that it felt like I could reach out and touch it.

Every so often a building appeared through the fog, and we would think it was the albergue. I kept getting relieved that the end was in sight and then heartbroken when each building turned out to be someone's house. As 1:00 p.m. neared, and more pilgrims passed us, I felt sure that they were going to take my reservation, and I resented them all. Nearly every pilgrim asked me if I was hurt. I fell again, and my knees hit the ground hard. Moaning in pain, I rolled over and slowly got back on my feet. My dark thoughts from the night before screamed inside my head. How can I complete the Camino if I cannot even make it up this hill? I hate this! I'm miserable and sore! What was I thinking coming out here? I was not even five miles into a five hundred mile journey.

We reached the albergue in Orisson at exactly 1:00 p.m. Beth met me at the door with a big hug and said, "Congratulations, you made it!" I immediately rushed over to the front desk where a woman checked me in and stamped my credential. The sound of the stamp was the most beautiful sound I heard all day. Every stamp on my credential represented one day more than I imagined I could walk. If I could survive my first day, maybe I could survive my second.

The woman walked me outside and around the back of the building. Rain was falling much harder now, and I felt lucky to have beaten the bulk of the storm. On the other side of the building was a flight of steps leading to the second floor that the woman quickly ascended. I grabbed onto the metal railing to pull myself up. My legs were feeling so heavy that lifting each foot took tremendous effort. On the fourth step, I slipped and fell down onto my side, and my pack rolled down to the bottom of the stairs. I tried to get up and slipped again, falling down to the bottom next to my pack. I hoped I could get to my feet before the woman noticed, but she heard the commotion and came rushing down in a panic.

"Oh my goodness, are you okay?" she exclaimed, in her strong French accent.

"I'm fine, I just tripped," I said, as I got to my feet.

She took my pack and carried it up the stairs as I pulled myself up with the railing. The room had ten sets of bunks, and as I expected, only top bunks were open. This was a problem on the Camino I had read about. Everyone wanted a bottom bunk, and it required arriving at the albergues before the crowds to secure one. I knew there was the possibility of asking someone to switch with me, but I did not particularly enjoy appearing needy to other people. Fortunately the beds were close together, and I was able to use the adjacent one as support to climb the ladder.

After settling in, I met an Australian man in his late forties named Ethan who was in the bunk next to me. His wild salt and pepper colored hair and dark rimmed glasses made him look like a college professor. I found it refreshing to talk to him since he was the first native English speaker I met since beginning the Camino. We talked a bit about our day, before I squeezed in a nap before dinner.

I woke up around 6:30 feeling very refreshed until I climbed down from my bunk and tried to walk. My legs were so stiff I could hardly bend my knees. I hobbled to the back porch to put my shoes on. The albergue was filled now, and everyone was bumping into each other as they organized their supplies and prepared for dinner. As I sat on a bench, Ethan approached and said, "Mr. America! Here are some other Americans for you."

Ethan pointed to an older husband and wife who appeared to be in their mid-seventies sitting on a bench by the back porch. They overheard our conversation and looked up at me. I slowly shuffled over to introduce myself. I was so exhausted that I had very little to say, even though I was overjoyed to finally meet someone from my own country.

When I entered the dining room downstairs, I found Beth, Alma, and Regina sitting at one of three long tables. After a difficult day, being among friends at my first sit-down meal of the Camino felt great. About forty pilgrims were seated in the dining room and before the food was served, everyone introduced themselves like students on the first day of school.

"Have you met Florence?" Alma asked, as she pointed to the stocky woman with short hair from Malaysia sitting next to me.

After a brief introduction, she talked about the trouble she was having and how her knee was hurting.

"I feel like the weakest person on the Camino. Everyone passes me. I don't think I can make it to Santiago with this pain," Florence said, with a defeated tone.

I told her I had muscular dystrophy and the difficulty I was having.

"With your determination, there is no doubt you will make it to Santiago. I wish I was as strong as you. I do not think I can make it over the Pyrenees tomorrow," she said.

"You just have to take it one step at a time. That's the only way I made it here. If you can take a step, then you can take another, and so on and so on."

She seemed to take what I said to heart and replied, "You inspire me."

When I tried to cheer up Florence, I wondered if I believed my words. I, too, felt like the weakest person on the Camino and questioned why I was here and if I could make it much farther. Whether or not I believed what I told Florence, part of what I said was true. The only reason I made it to Orisson was by taking one step at a time.

Regina overheard the conversation from across the table and exclaimed, "Bryan is strong," as she made a muscle with each arm. I just laughed along as I quietly poured a glass of wine and helped myself to a serving of beans and roast chicken. Receiving attention from people thinking I was strong made me feel a bit uncomfortable. I thought to myself, "I know I'm weak. Are people telling me I'm strong just to make me feel better? Am I truly strong?"

Despite my personal emotions, the food tasted amazing, and the wine was even better. At the end of the meal, Alma pulled out her map, still damp from the rain, and we all studied tomorrow's route through the Pyrenees to Roncesvalles. There was a lot of steep trail ahead, but the worst seemed to be behind us. Alma said that she and Beth would like to walk with me tomorrow. She felt that we had met for a reason, and by walking slowly, I was allowing her to take in the surroundings and "experience the Camino as it was meant to be experienced."

I felt touched by Alma's statement and was surprised that someone enjoyed walking slowly and even enjoyed the Camino more with me. My fears from the night before were beginning to dissipate, and it was thanks to Alma and Beth's willingness to help. After dinner I went outside with Florence and Regina now that the rain and fog had lifted. Scattered white clouds moved slowly across the mountaintops. The wet grass and trees glowed a vibrant green. Tucked away in the valleys were irrigated pastures with grazing livestock. On several mountainsides were small peaceful homes with traditional European red clay shingles. Buildings from the outskirts of St-Jean were faintly visible to the far left on the horizon, allowing for a perspective on how high I had climbed. In just over five hours, I achieved around two thousand feet of elevation gain.

"And how are you feeling now after your first Camino meal, Mr. America?" Ethan asked, as he joined us.

"Great! Still feeling a little stiff, but that good meal should help," I said.

"Have you met Angie?" Ethan asked, as he introduced me to a girl who had just walked up. Angie was from Germany and walked with Ethan from St-Jean that day. She was a little older than me, with reddish-brown hair, a radiant smile, and a strong German accent. Our conversation did not move beyond initial greetings. We were all too tired to make pleasant talk. After taking in the view, I said goodnight to Beth and Alma, and we agreed to meet tomorrow morning by 7:00.

Back in the dorm area as I prepared for sleep, I met a blond-haired American girl in her mid-twenties from Michigan named Jillian. She was dressed in a white shirt and pink pajama pants, and sitting on her bed organizing a pile of clothes. Beside her was an enormous backpack bulging with enough supplies for two people.

"How hardcore of a hiker are you? Did you even bring deodorant?" she asked, as she pulled a full size deodorant and shampoo bottle out of her backpack, and several other bottles and toiletries of unknown content fell out along with them.

"I just brought small travel-size containers," I said.

"I think I brought too much stuff," she said, with heavy eyes as she held up a second pair of sneakers and two jackets.

"Have you ever been on a hiking trip before?" I asked.

Jillian had a look of regret and said, "No. I'm thinking maybe this wasn't the right thing for me to do." She complained of knee and back pain caused by her heavy pack. A few days later I heard that Jillian had dropped out and headed home. I hoped I would not have a similar fate and story that circulated among the pilgrims. The added weight I carried was not in my pack but in the uncertainty of my body's ability.

I slept well that night despite the excessive snoring that I was mostly able to block out with the earplugs I was advised to bring. Finishing the day felt like an incredible accomplishment. Though I had only walked five miles with almost five hundred more still to go, completing the first day accounted for a distance that could not be measured in mileage.

I was on the trail with my newly formed group by 7:30 on the morning of my second day. Alma held to her promise from yesterday and continued walking with me, while Beth and Regina immediately went past us. The initial trail out of Orisson only had a slight incline and continued along a paved road. Having level ground to begin the day allowed my muscles to warm up before we reached harder sections. Today was foggy again with only a few feet of visibility, and the change in elevation brought an obvious drop in temperature. For most of the day the trail followed along a ridgeline overlooking a forested valley.

As the fog continued to clear throughout the morning, hundreds of grazing sheep could be seen on the hilltops. They looked elegant, moving in flocks as a single unit. As one flock moved past us, we stopped to take a few pictures with an older couple in their mid-seventies. They introduced themselves as Tom and Lucy from South Carolina. Tom was sitting on a rock putting a brace on his knee, which was already in pain. They began in St-Jean and were heading to Roncesvalles on their first day. Initially, they did not look like people one would find walking the Camino, but I quickly learned that age meant nothing when it came to willpower. Tom and Lucy were dressed in a similar manner with short pants, light sweatshirts, bandanas, and matching hiking poles. Lucy's bandana had a map of the Camino on it, and Tom joked how they were relying on it if they ever became lost. A few years before, they walked the Camino from León to Santiago. Now they were walking from St-Jean to León, so they could say they walked the entire route. Our new acquaintances joined us, and around noon we all stopped for a rest and lunch near a food truck parked along the road. This was a busy place as more pilgrims from St-Jean were passing through. After eating, Alma and I continued to rest while Tom and Lucy ventured ahead.

From here, the Camino turned off the paved road and headed up a rocky path to an elevation of over 4,300 feet, the highest point of the Camino through the Pyrenees. I was at 574 feet in St-Jean, and realizing the amount the elevation changed in two days was incredible.

This section was only a couple hundred feet long but really challenged me. I relied on my hiking pole to keep my balance as I put both hands on the pole to push off and get both legs over large rocks. One boulder was too high to climb over with my pack on, so I took it off and handed it to Alma who grabbed my hand and pulled me up as I pushed off with my hiking pole.

After putting my pack back on, I was able to get up the last portion of the trail on my own. My heart was racing, and I was nearly out of breath when I reached the top. During my first night in St-Jean, when I struggled to walk up the road, the thought of crossing the Pyrenees seemed impossible, but now the worst was behind me. From the top, the view was obscured by dense fog that had moved in. With no landmarks to see, it felt like we were at the top of the world.

On our descent, we began walking with a woman from California named Hazel. She had quit her job, was traveling the world, and recently arrived in Europe after being in

South America for several months. Hazel looked to be in her late thirties but had a bubbly personality and long hair that reminded me of someone a decade younger. She moved ahead quickly, but like so many others I met, I would see her again soon.

The rest of the day was relatively easy and downhill with only a few steep sections. We arrived in Roncesvalles shortly after crossing the Spanish border and met Beth and Regina at the albergue around 5:00. Once we checked in, we ventured into town to find a restaurant for dinner. I ordered a bocadillo jamón, which is basically a ham sandwich served on baguette. The meat, from black Iberian pigs, was cured, cut into thin slices, and sometimes tough and stringy. This delicious salty sandwich would become a staple meal for me.

As we were leaving the restaurant, we saw Florence, Ethan, Angie, and Hazel at an outside table enjoying a few drinks. Everyone congratulated me on making it this far, as by this point, word had spread that I had muscular dystrophy.

"Why don't we do a round of shots?" Ethan yelled out. He called over a server and ordered everyone a shot of absinthe.

"To making it over the Pyrenees!" Hazel called out, and we all repeated and downed the shot.

I felt completely immersed in the Camino community at this moment. I had already met so many amazing people in the first fifteen miles, and I knew this was only the beginning. The next goal was to reach Zubiri tomorrow.

3

PARTING WAYS

The next day's walk was relatively flat without a major mountain range to climb. I was able to easily keep up with the others. The villages we passed through had similar architecture as St-Jean with vibrant colors illuminated by the bright sun. All the locals at the cafés and on the streets smiled as we passed, and I could not help but smile back. As I looked around at the rural landscape with mountains on the horizon, I realized this was why I came to the Camino.

Despite the relative ease of the terrain, I was still tired after spending all day on my feet. That afternoon as we neared our destination in Zubiri, a steep section of trail caused a cramp in one of my calf muscles. At the top of a hill, I sprawled out on the ground from exhaustion and massaged my leg. As a child, I would often get leg cramps, but they became less frequent as I got older. I hoped these three days of difficult walking would not bring them back.

"Drink some water," Alma said, like a worried mother. We rested for a few moments, and I took a few sips of warm water. As we were getting ready to move, Ethan, Angie, and Hazel arrived. They had all been together since Roncesvalles. After chatting for a few minutes, they moved ahead, only to have us pass them a few minutes later while they were resting. This continued several times throughout the afternoon, and we joked about how different "Camino families" form along the way. Ethan explained how earlier that day someone thought Angie was his daughter. This was probably because they acted like two people who had known each other for a long time. The Camino had a way of creating strong, life-long friendships in an incredibly short time. Alma, Beth, and Regina were feeling like a mother and two sisters, and it made me sad to think that I might have to part ways with them soon. Regina was leaving tomorrow when she reached Pamplona, and Beth and Alma would need to increase their pace soon if they wanted to reach Santiago within their time frame. I wondered if I could find another group who would feel like a family.

I slept well that night at the albergue in Zubiri after having a big meal at a restaurant, but the next morning everything in my body hurt worse than after my first day. My legs felt like rubber, and I knew I could fall at any moment. As we left the albergue in the morning we passed a big tour group gathered and preparing for the day. This was the first of these groups I encountered on the Camino. Every day a bus picked them up at their hotel, dropped them off at their starting point. This practice felt like cheating when I had to rely on myself without an expensive tour company. I nodded hello to several people in the group as we passed by.

We encountered a slight hill shortly after leaving town. Along this section were piles of fresh horse manure. I made wide circles around several of them as the stench opened my sinuses. At the top of a hill, my shaky legs caused the inevitable as I tripped and fell. As luck would have it, I landed on a fresh wet pile. I yelled out in agony as my right leg and pants became covered in manure. My hands went down to catch my fall and were also coated in brown sticky matter. I brushed my hands in the grass along the side of the trail, and Alma helped me to my feet.

Two middle-aged women from the tour group, who sounded like they had Italian accents, rushed over as I tried to decide how to clean myself. Without asking if I needed help, one woman took a towel from her pack and the other pulled out her water bottle to wet the towel. My leg and hands were scrubbed clean in a matter of minutes. I offered them my sincerest thanks, and they continued on with the rest of their group.

While only a few moments before my fall, I felt disdain towards the tour group, it was amazing how rapidly my opinion changed. These strangers not only cleaned me but also taught me that you do not know anyone until they have a chance to demonstrate kindness. Once again, the Camino provided a lesson on the true nature of the journey to Santiago. From the poorest to the richest, and the strongest to the weakest, help was hidden everywhere.

Though I was glad to have survived the manure incident relatively unscathed, my falls for the day were not over. I fell four different times on a hill to Ilaratz, the first village we passed for the day. "Why is this happening to me?" I said after one of the falls, as Regina helped me to my feet.

"Just keep taking it slow," Alma said, undeterred.

On the paved road in the village, I fell again. I could see everyone looked concerned. In my mind, everyone's expression was saying, "We can't keep walking with him like this. He's slowing us down." Regardless of what I believed they were thinking, I could not keep falling like this all the way to Santiago. It was only a matter of time before I might sprain an ankle or break a bone. Everything I hid from my entire life was in front of me, and I could not run away. When no one was looking, I wiped a tear from my eye. Ilaratz was nothing more than a dozen buildings with traditional Basque architecture and a water fill station next to a few benches.

"Why don't you sit down and rest for a little while," Alma said. Under a shaded awning, the cool cement benches were a comfortable relief as the temperature was beginning to rise. There was a stickiness in the air where one could almost taste the heat of the day. As we were all resting, Ethan, Angie, and

Parting Ways

Hazel came up the hill. Ethan had a visible limp as he walked toward us and sat down. The sole of one of his sneakers was coming off causing him to walk differently and hurt his calf muscle.

"This is the last time I'll buy a pair of cheap sneakers," Ethan said, with a hopeless look. He tied a piece of string around his shoe to keep it together, but his calf injury was of more concern, and he was debating on taking a rest day soon.

Our group moved on after a few minutes, feeling refreshed and ready to take on the hot day. As we were leaving, a group of three Spanish women, who we met briefly the day before, arrived at the water station. We talked with them for a few minutes before we continued on. Every day there were new pilgrims to meet, and the Camino really did feel like a family stretched out across five hundred miles.

"Drink lots of water. You'll need it today," Hazel said, as we walked away.

As the day went on, the temperature climbed to almost one hundred degrees. Luckily, the next section was mostly through shade, but my heart was beating fast from exertion. We stopped for a short rest at the bottom of a hill near a small stream. The three Spanish women arrived shortly after and asked to take a picture with all of us. Though I could not understand what they were saying, their continuous laughter always brought a smile to my face. Their appearance was that of a group of women on a weekend stroll, wearing yoga pants, sneakers, and small daypacks. Regina translated to us that they began their walk in Roncesvalles a few days ago and were only walking to Pamplona to catch a bus home. Hazel caught up with us as we were leaving and explained how Ethan had stopped for a rest with Angie. His calf injury had become debilitating. Beth, Alma, and Regina sped up, so I walked with Hazel for a while. I felt like Beth and Alma needed to walk without me since Alma had been with me for nearly every moment of the Camino. Branching out and making other friends

27

was important since I felt my inevitable separation from Beth and Alma was looming closer.

As I walked with Hazel, I tripped and fell on a small incline and went down hard on my knees. My hiking pole fell out of my hands and Hazel had to do a little dance to avoid tripping over it. Hazel picked my pack up, and I got to my feet and brushed the dirt off my legs.

"I heard you have muscular dystrophy. You're strong for continuing on like you do," Hazel said.

"Thanks. Well, at this point I'm in this whether I like it or not. I'm not sure what the drive behind this is," I said.

"Come on, Bryan. We've all got something driving us to keep going," Hazel said.

"I don't know. I thought I knew, and now I don't think I know anymore. What drives you?" I asked.

Hazel paused for a moment before she responded, "The child in me. I grew up with dreams of traveling the world, but all I did was work. So here I am. Quit my job to see the world and live."

As I thought about her answer, I realized that the initial drive behind my journey was the fear that I would not be able to be someone like Hazel. I was afraid that my muscle weakness would prevent me from seeing the world and finding adventure. Maybe I could not do things the same as everyone else, but here I was hiking the Camino de Santiago.

As we approached the next small town of Zuriáin, with familiar rustic architecture, I began to feel dizzy from the heat. We stopped at the first café in town where Beth, Alma, and Regina were already sitting outside in the shade. Inside was a dimly lit room with a fan spinning from the ceiling and a short Spanish man standing behind the bar. I purchased my usual bocadillo jamón and joined everyone outside. A few minutes later, the Spanish women, Ethan, and Angie arrived. Sitting beneath the shade of the umbrellas brought relief, but sweat still dripped from my forehead.

Parting Ways

Hazel asked, "Are you feeling alright, Bryan?"

My face was bright red, and my heart was beating fast. I tried to sit still and took slow breaths to calm my nerves.

"You should go sit inside where it's cooler," Hazel said.

She brought me inside the air-conditioned café. I started with a glass of water and ended up drinking a liter and a half. Beth and Ethan came in and decided we all needed a long rest to avoid overheating. The breeze from the fan cooled me off, and my heart rate slowly returned to normal.

"I didn't want to make you nervous earlier, but you weren't looking very good," Hazel said.

That was probably the closest I ever came to heat exhaustion. I was learning there was so much more to contend with besides falls and tired muscles.

After our hour rest, Beth, Alma, Regina, and I said goodbye to Ethan, Hazel, and Angie and headed out on the last seven miles to Pamplona.

As we left Zuriáin, the trail followed the winding Arga River. This shallow river was surrounded by trees that provided much needed shade. The gravel trail eventually led past a deep swimming hole, so Beth and Regina decided to wade in and cool off while Alma took off her shoes and cooled her feet. The three Spanish women arrived while we were resting, and they jumped in too. I just wanted to get to Pamplona and be finished with this day. Alma and I decided to continue on while the others finished their swim and would catch up to us later. The trail turned away from the river and up a flight of cement steps. The white cement was almost blinding as it reflected the sunlight. I was prepared to drag my pack and crawl when Alma offered to help.

She gladly carried both our packs, as well as helping me up the steps. When we finally reached the top, a few tears rolled down my face. I could not believe how kind Alma was. How could I ever return her kindness? I wondered if I had ever shown that amount of kindness to someone. I knew the

Camino would have sections where help was necessary, but I never imagined the degree of unconditional help Alma would end up providing. This journey had become more than just me struggling all the way to Santiago, and evolved into the stories of others intertwining with mine. We had become an equal part of each other's Camino.

At the top, the view of arid rolling hills stretched out as far as I could see with a few outlying buildings of Pamplona visible. The trail followed the ridge until it went downhill and through a small graffiti-ridden tunnel under a highway. Coming out of the tunnel, there was another extremely steep hill. Alma carried my pack again without hesitation.

Beth caught up with us, but Regina was not with her. One of the Spanish women had gotten sick from the heat and was vomiting. Regina wanted to stay and help her, and said she would catch up. We found out later that Regina and the Spanish women took a taxi to Pamplona to find a doctor. The heat from the day had caused a casualty, and I knew how close I had come to having the same experience. Regina spent the night with a friend in Pamplona and went home to Madrid the next day.

Arriving in the bustling Pamplona that evening was overwhelming after spending four days in rural villages. The stuffy and crowded albergue was filled with snoring like I never heard before. As I lay in bed that night, my whole body ached. My collection of scrapes and bruises was becoming extensive. In the morning my hips were so stiff that any movement was painful. My mind flooded with fears that my body had reached the end of its physical abilities. After breakfast when we finally got out of the city, my hips were warmed up and moving well, but my pace was still incredibly slow. Today was going to be hotter than yesterday, so Beth decided to move ahead of us to get to our destination in Uterga faster.

I sensed tension between Beth and Alma when they spoke that morning. Alma was unhappy with the idea of

Parting Ways

Beth walking all seven miles of the day alone. The situation felt awkward, like I was the reason for the problem. Alma wanted to help me, but her desire to walk the Camino with her daughter was understandable. Now that Regina was no longer with us, Beth's decision to walk ahead felt like a line being drawn. Alma's commitment to walk with me this day was firm, but I sensed tomorrow would be different.

Outside of the city, the trail led into a seemingly endless expanse of open farmland with no shade. Midway through our morning, we passed through the village of Zariquiegui where we were able to rest inside a cool café for lunch. As Alma and I were leaving, I heard a man call my name. I looked up and saw Tom and Lucy from South Carolina, who we met during our second day. Both of them, who were dripping with sweat, dropped their packs on the ground, and sat at our table in a huff.

"I'll tell you what, this water is sweating out of me faster than I can drink it," Tom said, as he gave a firm pat on my shoulder.

"I was telling Tom that we're at the age where they warn people to avoid heat," Lucy laughed.

"Ah, that's all a bunch of mumbo jumbo. We'll make it where we have to," Tom said.

After chatting a bit about old age and people who should avoid heat, muscular dystrophy came up in the conversation.

"See Lucy, this proves my point. Anyone can do anything. Even a bunch of old farts like us," Tom said.

Tom gave me his business card and said, "You ever find yourself in South Carolina, give me a call. A brother of the Camino is a brother of mine."

We knew we would see them again soon because the trail was about to go over a large hill known as Alto de Perdón that would surely slow us down. At the top of the hill was a famous monument that portrayed twelve pilgrims walking to Santiago. The summit was just under a mile and a half away, but the trail was nearly as steep as the Pyrenees. With our water bottles topped off again, we continued our journey through the barren landscape.

The trail out of Zariquiegui was immediately uphill on loose rock that made me unsteady. Although the terrain was difficult, the real problem was the heat. My body was losing energy. I took a breath, took a few steps, paused for a moment and repeated this cycle. The sun felt like it was slowly cooking my brain, and my body would shut down at any moment. Alma followed slowly behind and every few minutes took my water bottle out of my pack and handed it to me, and I did the same for her. Both of us were so drained that the effort required to take off our pack to get a water bottle felt like a marathon. As I finished the last of my first liter I said to Alma, "We don't have enough water."

"I know," she replied bluntly.

We were only midway up the hill, and there was no place to refill until Uterga. A few hundred feet from the top was an old cement fountain trickling with slow drops of water. Our guidebooks noted that this water was not recommended for drinking. The fountain was called El Fuente Reniega and was associated with a tale of temptation. Legend has it that at this location Satan appeared before a pilgrim, who was dying of thirst, and offered water in return for his soul. The pilgrim refused, so Saint James appeared and provided the pilgrim with water for remaining faithful. Nothing about the water looked drinkable. After some serious thought, we decided drinking it was not worth the risk. Still, not to let an opportunity like this pass by, I soaked the water into my bandana and then tied it around my head for some cooling relief. While we were stopped at the fountain, Tom and Lucy approached us on the trail.

"Don't waste your time here. I heard there is a snack truck at the top of the hill that sells cold drinks," Tom said, as he hurried past us.

Parting Ways

Alma and I looked at each other with eyes lit up in excitement, and I thought to myself, "Here is Saint James appearing to us with water."

With thoughts of ice cold soda, I had a sudden burst of energy. Our decision to pass the forbidden fountain was about to be rewarded. As we neared the ridge, the spinning blades of wind turbines on the hill created a welcomed cooling breeze. When we finally made it to the top, there was a beautiful white truck parked alongside a worn-out paved road. Just as I was imagining what drink to buy, the truck began moving away and disappeared like a mirage in the desert.

"What? No!" I heard Tom's voice call out.

I turned and saw Tom and Lucy, who were taking pictures, walking over to us with hands up in the air and mouths wide open.

"Well, I guess we can't have everything," Lucy said, as she took a sip from her water bottle.

My gaze turned to the steel monument stretched out about seventy-five feet across the ridgeline. Twelve pilgrims were depicted making the pilgrimage to Santiago, some on foot and others on horseback. Though they were rusted and marked with graffiti, they demonstrated how much harder the journey was for pilgrims a millennium ago. Ancient pilgrims were lucky to eat every day and faced dangers of bandits and plague. As difficult as my Camino was, it was always comforting to realize how much easier the pilgrimage had become over the centuries.

Tom and Lucy, along with several other pilgrims, moved on after a few minutes. I did not know if I would see them again since they were walking to Puente la Reina, which was another four miles farther than the two miles Alma and I needed to reach Uterga. There was a small cement structure nearby that offered the only shade for miles, so we sat to rest for a few minutes and imagined our warm water was cold soda. The view from the top of the hill was worth the difficult walk. Patches of farmland and villages scattered the vast expanse of land. Pamplona lingered on the horizon, and what was to be the last view of the Pyrenees Mountains still stood as a reminder of the challenge I had overcome. The mountains looked greenish-blue on the horizon, a stark contrast to the brown and yellow landscape we just walked through. On the other side of the ridge, Uterga was clearly visible just past the descent. Beyond the town were a few scattered hills among farmland, but there were no mountains on the horizon of clear blue sky.

After a few minutes of rest, Alma and I continued on to Uterga. We each had about a half liter of water, just enough to reach our destination and not succumb to heat stroke and dehydration. The path down from the ridge was steeper than the way up, with loose sharp rocks and no firm ground. It felt like I was walking on marbles. After a few steps, my feet went out from under me, and I fell down hard on my rear end. The rocks were hot to the touch and dug into my knees as I struggled to stand.

"I don't know how I'm going to make it down here," I said to Alma, as she handed my pack back to me when I got to my feet.

"I will hold on to you," Alma said.

As we continued down, she held tightly onto my pack to make sure I fell down easily and did not break a wrist or an ankle. Help was essential through this section, and it required every bit of concentration I had, but I still fell nearly a dozen times. With every fall, the thought crossed my mind that this was where I would finally get hurt and not be able to get back up, but I kept moving forward. I felt a drive like nothing I had ever felt before.

I thanked Alma for holding on to me, and she said, "I think I'll be worried about you when we finally part ways."

Every part of the journey was done with Alma as my guide, and I rarely opened by guidebook. My experience on the Camino thus far was lacking self-reliance. My only experience on the trail was with this group. Soon I would be alone.

At the bottom of the rocky hill, we still had another forty-minute stretch to Uterga. By this point I had more water than Alma, so I gave her some of mine. Any way I could help her, I made sure to do after all she did for me. I realized how rare it was to find someone who not only helped me but acted as a mother and gave more than she received. She was sweating profusely and sat to rest on a large rock as she took a sip of water. I stopped with her, but she wanted me to continue, and she would catch up after her rest.

"Are you sure you don't want me to stay with you while you rest?" I asked, one last time.

"No! Keep going!" she snapped.

Her harsh tone caught me off guard, and I hurried off without saying another word. We had been together almost continuously for five days, and everyone has changes in moods during any extended amount of time, especially in extreme heat. Still, I knew the change in tone was a sign that my pace was too slow and walking together was not going to be practical much longer.

Farther up the gravel trail, just as Uterga came into view, I found a white statue of the Virgin Mary on the side of the trail under the shade of a large tree. A long cement bench was in front of the statue, so I sat down and gazed at the statue. I realized how little thought I had given to the religious aspect of the Camino. I was on a walk to see the tomb of Saint James and was not even sure what God was. In my childhood I was raised Catholic by my mother but never continued to practice after my sacraments. Terms like "agnostic" or "spiritual but not religious" were what I used to describe myself. The countless churches along the Camino occasionally made me think about my Catholic past, but I never ventured inside of them. I had no plans of having a religious transformation on the Camino, but I wondered if my feelings on religion would change on this journey. With the mindset of being an explorer, I was always open to new wisdom on how the world worked. Maybe the Camino would teach me something beyond simply dealing with physical weakness.

As I stared longer at the statue of the Virgin Mary, I decided to truly pray for the first time in my life. "Well, I don't know if anyone is there or if anyone is listening, but I just wanted to say a few words to you. Alma has been such a huge help, but I know my time with her and Beth is coming to an end. I hope someone else can take their place. Going on alone is so scary for me. I don't know if you can do something for me, but I hope everything you do for me has some purpose. All this pain must mean something, and I hope you have a plan for me, whatever it is," I said, as tears formed in my eyes.

This moment alone was important. I would not have spoken those words if someone was with me. Maybe there was a message to be found on the Camino, or maybe the long day in the heat was making me crazy. After sitting for a few minutes in silence, looking at the emotionless face of the statue, I heard footsteps approach from behind. I turned to see Alma standing next to me with a large smile.

"Let's continue on, shall we?"

The time alone gave us both a much needed boost in our spirits. As we passed the first few buildings in Uterga, Alma received a text message from Beth. Alma was feeling light-headed and having blurry vision. Her speech sounded confused, and she was having trouble operating her phone. This confirmed my worries from when I left Alma to rest alone. She was experiencing some of the first signs of heat exhaustion. I could not read Norwegian but spelled out the words to her. We understood that Beth had a room reserved for three people and was waiting for us. Alma needed to be somewhere cool immediately. As we approached the albergue, Beth greeted us with two large glasses of iced lemonade, and we sat down in the shade of a patio. Saint James had finally arrived.

Parting Ways

Both Alma and I were in bliss knowing that our walk through the heat was finished. I collapsed into a chair and closed my eyes. There are few better feelings I have experienced in life than finally sitting down after walking all day. The pins and needles feeling in my feet and muscles slowly began to dissipate.

As Alma, Beth, and I sat outside in the shade of the albergue courtyard sipping our drinks, I saw a man in his mid-sixties sitting on a lawn chair. He had a thick head of dark grey hair, a clean shaven face, and a dark tan. Dressed in tan cargo shorts, a white t-shirt, and flip flops, it was evident he came from a warm climate. After overhearing us talking about the heat, the man chimed in and said the temperature reached one hundred six degrees, and the heat wave was expected to last another five days. Recognizing his American accent, I asked him where he was from. His name was Connor, and he was from Florida.

"Me and my wife Evelyn are used to the heat, but today was too much for us. We started in Zariquiegui this morning and could not go any farther."

After resting for a few minutes, Alma and I walked inside to check in. The spacious dimly-lit entry room with red-tiled floor had several tables and couches. A pretty girl a couple years older than me with blond hair, fair skin, and blue eyes sat on one of the couches reading a book. As I waited at the front desk, she looked up and said with a bright smile, "Looks like you had a hell of a day."

"Yeah," I laughed and said, "And the best part is that I get to do it all again tomorrow."

She laughed and said, "Well, relax now. Maybe I'll see you at dinner. My name is Ella, by the way."

"I'm Bryan. It's nice to meet you," I said, as she returned to her reading.

Ella sounded American with a slight Scandinavian accent. I did not ask where she was from because she seemed preoccupied, but she was very attractive and friendly, and I hoped to talk with her later.

Once I was checked in, we went to our room and I immediately lay down in bed and fell asleep. Around 6:45 p.m., Beth woke me up for dinner, exclaiming, "Florence is here! Come down to eat." I knew she was talking about Florence from Malaysia who I met during my first Camino meal in Orisson four days earlier. Our conversation about how defeated she felt at the end of the first day seemed like a distant memory after all I had been through.

The dining room was packed with almost thirty pilgrims sitting at four long tables. I saw Connor sitting at a table with his wife, along with Ella and two middle-aged women. Initially I thought to sit with Connor and Ella to begin meeting some new pilgrims, but I had little choice. Beth led me over to another table where a seat was saved for me next to Florence. As soon as Florence saw me, she jumped up and gave me a huge hug.

"Bryan! I can't believe you made it this far! You did it!" she exclaimed.

"I still have a long way to Santiago," I said, still not fully awake from my nap.

"You'll make it there. I just know it."

I sat down at the prepared table setting and helped myself to a roll and a glass of red wine. The meal was brought out moments later. The thick vegetable soup and chicken tasted so good after not eating since a dry bocadillo jamón earlier that afternoon. I easily drank two generous glasses of the smooth wine, making me even more ready for sleep.

As I had foreseen, the dinner conversation shifted to a subject I wished to avoid but was inevitable. Beth and Alma realized they needed to pick up their pace if they were going to make it to Santiago by their deadline. They were already farther behind than they would have liked, and our current pace could not continue anymore.

Parting Ways

Florence suggested Beth and Alma rent bikes for an upcoming section of the Camino known as the Meseta because it would be relatively flat, and they could make up some time. Beth seemed excited about this idea, but I kept quiet during this conversation. Part of me felt mad at myself for wishing I could stay with them. I realized it was selfish to rely on Alma for her help and knowledge of the Camino. Attachment was something I needed to avoid if I was going to use the Camino as an experience to grow. Alma had already given me more than I ever imagined, and I could ask no more from her. This was probably a good time and place for us to part ways. The terrain would become easier over the next few days, and I would require less help.

I went upstairs when I was done eating, but Beth and Alma stayed a little longer and talked to Florence. The day's heat had drained me of all my energy. Shortly after Beth and Alma came up to sleep, Alma sat down on her bed and said, "Bryan, I think tomorrow morning we will separate. I've had a nice time helping you, but we need to move ahead. I know you will find someone else to help you."

Alma's face looked like a lot of thought had gone into her words. Her lack of eye contact revealed this decision hurt her as much as it hurt me. There was no reason for resentment. I was discovering that the Camino was a personal journey, and everyone needs to walk for themselves and make the decisions they feel are right. Still, I felt crushed inside, but I agreed with Alma that it was time for us to part ways.

As I went to sleep, I felt a fear similar to what I felt during my first night in St-Jean: a hopeless feeling that I could not continue without the help of others. The difference between this night and my first night was that I had now walked fifty-three miles and crossed the Pyrenees Mountains. I knew a series of challenges awaited me over the next four hundred fifty miles, but I would worry about that tomorrow. Sleeping is always the best way to take your mind off something.

4
JAKSAA, JAKSAA!

Beth's phone alarm went off at 5:30 a.m., and I jumped awake from a deep sleep. I had already packed the night before, so I just rolled out of bed, put my shoes on, and threw my pack over my shoulders. Beth and Alma were still fumbling around and organizing everything. I told them I would be waiting outside for sunrise, so we could say our goodbyes there. Since this was my first day alone, I was fearful of venturing out into the dark. Even with a headlamp, I was afraid of getting lost. I would not have Alma's knowledge of the route anymore.

My legs felt shaky as I walked down from our room to the lobby. Walking down steps with my heavy pack was probably the most dangerous thing I did on the Camino. I always made sure to take my time. Getting an injury on stairs would be depressing after all the rough terrain I walked over. Usually my hiking pole was a great help to maintain balance, but as I tried to adjust my pole, it was stuck in place. The heat and dust from the day before made everything tight.

In the lobby I saw Ella sitting with the two middle-aged women she ate dinner with last night. They were all sitting on a bench organizing their gear. Ella was wearing black yoga shorts, a black tank top, and her hair was pulled back under a blue bandana. The other two women were dressed in light clothing and had rough weathered looks. One woman was a bit older with short grey hair and smiled at me as I came down the steps. The other, with short brown hair and sunglasses resting on her head, did not look up as I approached. She was rubbing cream on her knees and had a defeated expression in her face.

"Hey! Good morning," Ella said.

"Good morning. Buen Camino," I said, as I opened the front door and paused for a moment. Perhaps I could ask Ella to unlock my hiking pole, instead of waiting for Beth and Alma's help. Asking women I do not know to help me with tasks that require strength always feels awkward. Usually men are seen as stronger, and women are often initially confused by my lack of strength. I have lost count of the number of times girls have asked, "You're a strong man, can you open this for me?" and then having an embarrassing interaction of not being able to help. Already this stereotype was beginning to bother me less on the Camino after being put in situations where I accepted any help available.

"Can one of you help me unlock my pole? I can't seem to get it," I said.

The woman with sunglasses looked up, pointed to Ella and said in an American accent, "She's the strongest of us. She'll do it."

I handed Ella the pole, and she gave a strong twist and it unlocked.

"Thank you so much," I said.

"Of course, glad to help," Ella said, as I continued outside to wait for Beth and Alma.

I sat down on a cement bench along one of the courtyard walls and looked up at the clear sky still dotted with several stars. There was a humid breeze that suggested another hot day. The sounds of chickens cooing in the yard next to the albergue was a relaxing sound during the morning stillness. My thoughts focused on the day ahead, how I would manage alone, and who I might walk with. I looked back at the albergue and saw Ella and her group still packing. Maybe I could join them. Ella's friendliness and willingness to help unlock my hiking pole showed she might be a good walking partner. Hopefully Alma and Beth would come outside before Ella and her group left. Having a proper goodbye with my companions was more important than who I ended up walking with.

Beth and Alma arrived a few minutes later, and I stood up to meet them.

"Well, this is goodbye I guess," Beth said.

"I guess so," I said, as Beth gave me a hug.

I turned to Alma who had tears in her eyes and said, "We may cross paths again on this journey."

"We may. But I will miss your company," Alma said, as I gave her a hug.

"I will miss you both as well. Thanks for all your help," I said.

"Your spirit has helped me more than you know. Thank you," Alma said.

As we said our final goodbye and Alma and Beth did their last preparations before beginning their day, Ella and her group came outside.

I walked over to Ella and asked, "Hey is it alright if I walk with you guys? At least until the sun rises."

"Of course you can!" Ella said.

"Where are you guys from?" I asked.

"Finland," she said, as I thought how funny it was that I went from walking with one group of Scandinavians to another. Perhaps in some regard this was not completely by chance. This friendliness and willingness to help seemed to be related to Scandinavian culture. Initially I was surprised when Ella said Finland since her accent told a different story.

"I'm from New Jersey in the United States," I said to Ella.

"My mother lives in the States too. She's from Washington State," she said, as she pointed to the woman with sunglasses

Jaksaa, Jaksaa!

who had stopped to tie her sneakers at one of the tables in the courtyard.

"My mother is Hanna, and my mother's friend here is Lotta," Ella said, as she introduced the older woman who said hello, but it was obvious she spoke little English. Ella and Lotta spoke to each other in Finnish as we waited for Hanna. Finnish sounded unlike any European language I had ever heard. The accent was clearly Baltic, but the words sounded comparable to something from Asia.

Hanna walked over and said, "Okay, I think I'm ready."

"So you're from Washington? I'm from New Jersey," I said to Hanna, as we started walking.

"It's nice to meet another American. I was born in Finland but have lived in the U.S. for the past thirty years. My daughter Ella is American too, but moved to Finland a few years ago," Hanna said.

This explanation answered my questions about Ella's accent. Still, I found it odd that Ella introduced herself as Finnish first when she was from the United States. Why did she not want to identify herself as American? I had a feeling there was more to this story.

"Who were those people you were saying goodbye to?" Ella asked.

I explained how I had been with Beth and Alma for the past five days, and that I had muscular dystrophy and relied on their help.

"What type of muscular dystrophy do you have?" Ella asked.

This question surprised me. Usually people have no idea what muscular dystrophy is, and never ask what type.

"Becker muscular dystrophy," I said.

Hanna then joined the conversation and asked Ella, "Isn't that what my brother's children have?"

"No, they have nemaline myopathy," Ella said.

"Oh, yeah, that is a very different form than mine."

My Own Pace

Ella continued to explain, "Yeah, I'm a nurse. I know a little about your condition. How have you managed this far? That's incredible."

"A lot of willpower and help from others," I answered.

"That is very brave of you," Ella said.

Hanna said, "My Camino has been a lot like yours. I have very bad arthritis, and I'm in a lot of pain while walking, especially over hills and mountains."

"Well, it's nice to know I'm not the only person out here struggling with physical limitations," I said.

I remembered the prayer I said the day before at the statue of the Virgin Mary. This new group seemed to be the answer I was looking for. These were not only people who were willing to help, but people who understood my struggle.

The paved road out of Uterga led to a rocky dirt trail, and I immediately lost my footing and fell hard. This was exactly how I did not want to begin walking with a new group. Even with the light of my headlamp I had trouble seeing the loose rocks. We were surrounded by farmland, away from the lights of town. Ella immediately rushed over and helped me to my feet. After thanking Ella and assuring everyone I was alright, I continued walking. Minutes later, I fell again. Even in the darkness, I could see concern in everyone's face as Ella helped me up a second time.

"I'm just having trouble seeing the loose rocks in the dark. I don't usually fall this much," I laughed nervously. I did not want them to think my walk with them would be a constant series of falls.

"Well, we can walk slower with you. It's alright," Hanna said, reassuringly, but I could tell she was unsure of her commitment.

Hanna and Ella kept talking to Lotta in Finnish translating everything I said. In my mind they were plotting in secret to not walk with me anymore. Even though I understand why Beth and Alma left me, I felt that everyone I wanted to walk with was going to leave. A few minutes later I fell again. I was really embarrassed. The number of bruises on my body had been increasing over the past few days, and this morning was not helping. As I struggled to get back on my feet I said, "You guys can go on ahead if you want, and I will wait here for more light."

For a moment I considered that maybe I should just cut my losses and accept I was on the rest of this journey alone. However, Ella was firm in her words and said, "No, we will stay with you." I was unsure if Hanna and Lotta felt the same way.

After my third fall with the new group, the path became less rocky, making for easier walking, and a beautiful sunrise brought light to the landscape. No matter how dark it feels, sunrises always make things better, if only for a moment. The change in terrain gave me a chance to prove to these new companions that I was capable of keeping up. As the four of us made our way down the road, we were suddenly confronted by Beth and Alma heading toward us at a brisk pace.

"We must have gone the wrong way. The trail dead ends in a farmer's field," Beth said, with her head down looking at a map on her phone.

Hanna and Lotta went ahead with Beth and Alma as we backtracked. Ella walked slowly with me in the rear and said, "I feel bad that you had to walk all this way only to turn back."

"This was just the warm up for the day," I laughed.

"At least we only walked twenty minutes out of the way instead of two hours," Ella said.

Ella always had a genuine smile that revealed her kind soul. Having someone you hardly know help you up from a fall quickly builds a feeling of connection. This was why parting ways with Beth and Alma was so difficult. I hoped my new friendship with Ella would lead somewhere good.

We soon came to the fork in the trail that we had missed.

The marker clearly pointed the correct direction, but in the dark it was not visible. From difficult terrain to hidden paths, my apprehension of walking in the dark was justified. Beth and Alma said goodbye and continued on, disappearing around a bend. I found it interesting how separate their path had become from mine. In that interaction they could have been any other pilgrim, but my journey so far had been dominated by their presence. Now my Camino went on without them.

Back on the correct trail, I tripped on a rock and fell again. Feeling relaxed to be on the right path, my guard was down, and I was not watching for every bump in the trail. This time I looked down to see a gash on my knee and blood running down my leg. I felt like a little kid who skinned his knees playing kickball at recess. Just as fast as I fell down, Ella took off her pack and whipped out her medical kit.

"Here is some antiseptic. It will prevent infection and stop the bleeding," she said, as she applied it onto my scrape. There was a sting as the cream touched the open wound.

Ella took a bandage out of her pack and gave it a shake before she opened the wrapper and placed it over the cut.

"Keep it covered and you should be alright. Do you have fresh bandages?"

"Yes, I do."

"Put a fresh one on it tonight," Ella said.

"Thanks," I said, as Ella helped me to my feet, and I adjusted my pack.

The trail meandered through farmland until we came into the town of Muruzábal. This small town was surprisingly developed with modern homes, groomed hedges, and swimming pools. The dirt road immediately led onto freshly paved blacktop. We looked for a café to find some breakfast, but nothing was open. In Spain, an early start was bad for finding a meal. Coming out of Muruzábal, Hanna and Lotta stopped to take some trail mix out of their pack to eat as we walked.

Jaksaa, Jaksaa!

"Do you guys mind if I keep walking with you?" I asked.

"Not at all!" Ella said, without hesitation.

I did not want to appear like I elected myself as an integral member of their group. If I was going to walk with someone, I wanted them to choose to walk with me. Now that my falling had stopped and the terrain was flat, I felt less of a nuisance.

There was a downhill section after leaving Muruzábal, and then another gravel road through more farmland and tall dry grass. The open land between each village was refreshing, since where I lived in New Jersey had no separation between the continuous sprawl of suburban developments.

After crossing through a graffiti-ridden tunnel beneath a highway, we were met with a steep hill on a concrete road into the next town of Obanos. Everyone walked ahead on the hill and thoughts about them leaving me returned. At the top, Hanna and Lotta continued walking, but Ella stopped and waited as I climbed. The feeling of being at the bottom of a hill when everyone else is at the top was always so frustrating. Though the heat of the day had not fully kicked in, the humidity was making it difficult to breathe, and I began to sweat.

"I don't know how you do it, even after the first fall I would have had a hard time picking myself up and continuing. You are so strong, mentally and physically," Ella said, as I stopped to catch my breath.

"I don't know. I'm afraid I might not have the strength to reach Santiago," I said.

"Real strength comes from facing your fears. If you've made it this far, you certainly have the strength."

"Thanks for walking with me," I said, as we reached the top.

"Of course! And thanks for wanting to walk with me," Ella said.

Ella and I continued down the narrow street through the town until we caught up to Hanna and Lotta who were anxiously looking for an open café, but still the town was not

47

awake. We wandered through the quiet streets hoping to find something open, but as quickly as we entered the town we were back onto a dirt trail. From the other side of town, the road led along the ridge of a hill. The view from the slight elevation gain revealed patches of farm fields over rolling hills like waves in the ocean. The farms were so ancient and embedded in the landscape that they were an almost natural feature.

The trail through the open land followed a nearby highway and led us into the next town of Puente la Reina around 9:00. Life was finally beginning to awaken as we entered the town. Cars were driving along the highway and shops and stores were opening their doors. Along the main road we encountered the first open café of the day.

"Thank God. A Finn without her morning coffee isn't something you want to experience," Hanna joked, as her pace quickened, and we headed toward the small roadside café with tables and chairs set up in front.

While we ate breakfast, we could feel the temperature rising and discussed wanting to finish our day's walk as soon as possible. We had already covered four miles since Uterga, so we put our sights on the village of Lorca, which was about eight miles away.

Once we were back on the road into bustling Puente la Reina, I heard someone yell my name from behind. Wondering who it was, I turned to see Tom and Lucy.

"How are you, brother?" Tom said, as he shook my hand firmly.

"I'm great! Tired of this heat, but great!" I said.

"Where is the Norwegian woman you were walking with? Alma?" Tom asked.

"I parted ways with her this morning. She and her daughter moved on ahead of me. I was going a little too slow for them."

"Slow? There is no such thing as slow on the Camino;

Jaksaa, Jaksaa!

there is only your own pace. We all have our own difficulties, and we all deal with them in our own ways," Tom said.

Tom's words resonated with me for the rest of the Camino. Focusing on my own pace would become my mindset as other pilgrims came in and out of my journey. Feeling sad about leaving Beth and Alma was natural, but everyone has their own path to follow. The difficulty people have in focusing on their own pace in life relates to the problem of understanding strength. Most people, including myself, see themselves as weak in comparison to someone who is stronger or more physically capable. On the Camino, I was starting to realize that the idea of being weak only holds true when we compare ourselves to others. When we face challenges from our own unique reference point and not through the eyes of others, we become truly strong. Despite my realization that strength is a point of view, I could not help but wonder how physically strong I was for someone with my condition. An analogy I heard before of an ant carrying a seed being the equivalent of a human carrying a car came to mind. I had become the ant, accomplishing something that should be impossible on paper.

On a wide section of trail after town, my foot got caught on one of the rocks, and I went down. The fall was graceful and little more than a stumble, but I heard Tom call out my name while I was on the ground. Tom had yet to witness me fall and panicked. As I got to my feet, I turned to see Tom headed over to me in a quick jog.

With a sigh of relief that I was alright, Tom said, "Promise me you won't make an old man run like that again," as he caught his breath. Tom and Lucy went on ahead after my fall. I would not see them again for the rest of the Camino.

As I started walking again, Ella said, "We have a saying in Finnish, 'jaksaa, jaksaa' which means to have enough strength to continue further. So when you need to dig deep and keep going you say jaksaa, jaksaa."

"Jaksaa, jaksaa," I said, as I kept pushing up the hill.

My Own Pace

"I thought about that when you got up from your first fall this morning, and I think that represents the strength I see in you," Ella said.

When I spoke that phrase it flowed naturally. In a place where I had to find inner strength and receive help from people of other cultures, there were no better words to describe my Camino. With every fall I was searching for strength to stand up again and keep moving forward. Now there was a phrase to describe that struggle.

Continuing on from Puente la Reina, the trail became extremely steep as it moved through a small pine forest. Just like every other hill, I took small steps, advancing my feet a few inches at a time. Ella continued to walk slowly next to me offering words of encouragement as we moved along. Every so often Hanna and Lotta went ahead and sat on a log or rock and waited for us.

As we were climbing, I heard another voice from behind call my name. I turned and saw Florence. She was one of the few people I met during my first days who were still walking the Camino at the same pace as me. Her knee was still sore, and she was concerned about being able to finish the Camino. Florence made use of a backpack transfer service to send her pack ahead to Lorca where she was spending the night too. All of her day's supplies were put in a small drawstring bag she was wearing.

"Where's Beth and Alma?" Florence asked, as she looked around at who I was walking with.

"We separated this morning. They're a ways ahead of me now."

I introduced Florence to Ella who remembered seeing her at the albergue the night before. Florence began going on and on to Ella about how brave I was to be walking the Camino. Although I appreciated Florence's kind words, being an inspiration was difficult as I questioned if I could make it over this hill. Within the past hour the heat gained in intensity.

50

Jaksaa, Jaksaa!

Sweat dripped down my forehead and my legs became tired and heavy. Ella, who was watching me closely, was aware of the change in my mood and suddenly said, "Here, give me your pack."

She put it on the front of herself and held out her arm for me to link with and started pulling me up the hill. With the weight of both packs and the weight of me, I could feel the muscles in Ella's arm clench, and she put all her strength into this endeavor.

Florence linked with my other arm after a few moments, and they both pulled me up the hill. The ground began to flow beneath me as the help allowed me to move at a normal pace. Making it up the hill without help was possible, but Ella and Florence chose to make the journey easier for me. The strength I found on the Camino did not have to simply come from within. These people were giving me strength.

"Jaksaa, jaksaa," I reminded myself as we made it to the top of the hill.

I offered to take my pack back. I could see Ella struggling to carry both packs, but she said, "No, you need a break."

Eventually Florence took the pack from Ella and carried it for a while since she had no pack. Despite her hurt knees, she was still willing to give Ella a rest from carrying both packs. After a few minutes of flat ground there was another short hill. Ella linked arms with me again, and Florence still carried my pack. As we crested the top, we found Hanna and Lotta sitting on a boulder waiting for us. Hanna was experiencing some joint pain because of her arthritis and needed a rest.

I sat down on the boulder with Florence and Ella and drank some water. After a few minutes, Florence decided to continue walking and picked up my pack.

"You can leave my pack here," I said.

"It's alright, I can carry it to the next town for you," Florence said.

"I appreciate it, but I'll just keep my stuff with me."

As Florence walked away, Hanna said, "That girl worries about everyone else but herself. That's not going to help her make it anywhere."

I did not say anything about Hanna's comment, but I was surprised by her negativity toward helping others. Florence's offer to carry my pack to the next town was a little strange, but I saw no reason to criticize her. Surely after the help Ella had given her, Hanna would have understood the benefit of helping others. Perhaps she was not at the same place in her journey as me, and the growing heat and her pain were not helping her mood. One particular aspect I noticed about Hanna was that she had not smiled all day and was not very talkative with Ella. Something else was going on that I did not understand.

Hanna did make one joke while we were resting, saying, "Don't you like how we *walk* the Camino? We don't. We prefer to just sit and rest."

After our rest I continued walking with my new group into the afternoon. Before our lunch break in the town of Cirauqui, Hanna needed to tend to a blister on the bottom of her foot. Ella took out her medical pack, and Hanna took off her sneaker and sock to reveal a large painful blister that looked debilitating. I turned away as Ella used the threading technique to drain the blister. This method required sticking a threaded needle through the blister and leaving the thread in place, allowing the blister to drain without removing the skin. Hanna was moaning in pain as Ella performed the procedure.

"If these blisters continue I'll go home. This isn't a religious pilgrimage for me. I don't need to put myself through this," Hanna said in a whiny voice. With a bandage on her foot, we continued on. I felt fortunate to have avoided blisters so far. With all I had to contend with, any pain I could avoid was good.

As we continued on to our destination in Lorca, the trail led down a series of old rocky steps. Lotta helped me down the first section, but still I tripped and fell from the weight of my pack. My hands hit the ground, and my palms scraped the gravel path. There was no blood, but they burned as I poured water on them to clean off the dirt. Lotta helped me to my feet, and I gave her a nod to let her know I was okay. I found it fascinating how easily you could communicate basic emotions without speaking the same language.

As I started walking again Ella asked, "Do you want me to carry your pack again?"

I hesitated for a moment. I still felt like a burden every time someone helped me, but this steep section would be dangerous to attempt while wearing my heavy pack.

"If you want to," I said.

"I want to," Ella said.

I will never forget the way Ella said, "I want to." I realized she sincerely wanted to help. She was someone I needed to walk with as long as the Camino would allow.

Lotta and Hanna went ahead, and Ella carried my pack and held my hand down the rocky steps. The way Ella willingly took my hand indicated it was not simply about helping my balance. This was the hand of someone who wanted to make it known that I was not alone in my struggle. The steps were in poor shape from centuries of use and required complete concentration to make sure each foot landed firmly. At the bottom, we caught up to Lotta and Hanna who were resting in a lone patch of shade beneath a tree. Hanna was in a lot of pain and needed a longer break, so Ella and I continued on to Lorca.

During this section of the trail, which leveled out after the hill, Ella and I talked a lot about our lives and what had led us to walk the Camino. Ella was twenty-seven years old and was born and raised by her Finnish parents in a small town in Washington. Her family were members of the Laestadian Lutheran Church, known for their tight knit communities and strict literal interpretation of the Bible. Despite protest from her family, when Ella turned eighteen, she left the religion and moved to Finland to escape the backlash. While initially only planning to live with a relative for a few months, Ella stayed in Finland to attend college and become a registered nurse. After graduation, she worked a few odd nursing jobs and had recently finished a year in Madrid, Spain, teaching English and learning Spanish. From what she explained, her relationship with her mother was still troubled, and the Camino was an attempt to heal some of these wounds. For Hanna, to be in Spain hiking a Catholic pilgrimage trail was rare for someone of her religion who rarely travels. Ella had a nursing job lined up in Finland when she finished the Camino, and until then, she described herself as being "homeless." I told Ella she was a free spirit to just pick up her life and replant herself anywhere. Ella laughed when I called her a free spirit and said, "Free? If you can even call it that. More of a damaged spirit."

"But maybe you have to be a little damaged to be free," I said.

"Maybe," Ella said with a serious expression.

Besides the issue of religion, Ella had a lot of qualms with the United States, materialism, and the idea of the American Dream, so she considered her life in Europe an escape. After living the majority of her adult life in Finland, she no longer identified herself as being an American, but her mother still introduced her as an American. I recalled this introduction Hanna gave Ella when I first met her and understood why this was a point of disagreement. Ella's belief about her identity showed that where we are born does not need to define who we are.

Before Lorca, we stopped at an outside café along the side of the road and sat under the shade of an umbrella to wait for Hanna and Lotta. The time was approaching 2:00, and we had about another mile to go, but the heat was really slowing us down. I just wanted to be finished with this day and resting in a soft bed.

Hanna and Lotta arrived at the café a few minutes later.

Jaksaa, Jaksaa!

We all talked about whether to stop for the day in the upcoming town of Lorca or continue farther. Lotta was feeling good and was trying to persuade everyone to push three miles farther to Villatuerta, but my mind was set on Lorca.

Coming into town, we faced the final big hill of the day. My pace had turned to a slow crawl in the heat, but Ella stayed with me and carried my pack. I could tell she wanted to be finished with the day. Lotta and Hanna went ahead, and we slowly climbed the hill. When we reached town and found the others sitting in the shade waiting for us, Hanna immediately pushed us to keep walking to find an albergue.

Lorca was the smallest town we encountered that day and had one narrow main street lined with adobe and brick buildings. We found an albergue at the far end of town. The inside was dimly-lit and cool with several long tables in the dining and entry room. I tried to untwist and collapse my hiking pole, but it was stuck in place from the heat. Ella offered to help me and was able to collapse it. I realized how funny it was that the day's journey began and ended with her helping me with my hiking pole.

I walked directly up to the check-in desk and bought a bed for the night. The rest of the group sat down at one of the tables to cool off and decide whether to stay or continue on, but the look of utter exhaustion in everyone's eyes showed the decision had already been made.

Before I was directed to my bed, I told Ella I would be back downstairs later to have dinner. Walking up to the third floor bedroom took the last of my energy. Thankfully I was given a bottom bunk. The albergue was sparsely filled, and by evening the room I was given only had four other pilgrims among ten beds. While I was resting and organizing my gear, a door to one of the private rooms connected to my room opened and Florence walked out. Her eyes looked heavy like she had just woken from a nap. She quickly said hello and went downstairs. A few minutes later she returned with a personal pizza she had bought for me. Her generosity was shocking. I thanked her for the pizza and for helping me earlier in the day, but she just smiled and nodded before disappearing in her room for the rest of the night.

After eating the small pizza, I showered, changed the bandage on my knee, and packed my gear for tomorrow. I heard a few Finnish voices in the hallway and looked out to find Ella and Lotta using the washing machine in the common area. They had a room with three beds down the hallway.

"How are you feeling?" Ella asked, as I walked into the area and sat on one of the three worn brown couches.

"Better now that I'm out of the heat."

"Yeah, I'm glad we decided to stop here," Ella said as I nodded my head in agreement.

The conversation ended quickly because we were both so tired, but I asked Ella, "Do you want to walk together tomorrow?"

"I'll have to see what my mother wants to do, but I had a nice time walking with you today. I hope we can do it again tomorrow," Ella said.

"Cool, let me know what you decide. I'll be around," I said.

As I got up to go back to my bed, Ella asked, "Do you want to get drinks later tonight?"

"Sure," I said.

"How does 7:00 sound?"

"Sounds good to me. I'll see you downstairs later."

After another short nap, I went downstairs to meet Ella. I ordered another personal pizza, and we both got beer. We sat quietly for a few minutes sipping our beer. Ella pulled her hair band off her head and ran her fingers through her hair before looking down into her glass of beer.

"Today was a hell of a day," I said.

"But you did great," Ella replied.

"Yeah, thanks. I just don't know if I can do this for another five weeks. The trail has been taking a toll on me. I don't know how many more bruises and cuts I can take."

"But you have such strength, more than I'll ever have. Don't let anything convince you otherwise," Ella said.

"Thanks. I mean, all I keep doing is putting one foot in front of the other."

"I guess that's all any of us can do," Ella said.

Ella apologized for what she felt was obvious tension between her and her mother. I said I had not noticed any, and Ella smiled a silent laugh knowing I was only being kind. The tension between the two of them did not feel like something I should involve myself with.

"Well, I will walk with you tomorrow. My mother and Lotta will walk ahead without us. I would much rather walk with you," she said, as she reached out across the table and touched my hand for a moment. She looked down at the table with a serious expression.

I was unsure how to read the way she interacted with me. Was the affection she demonstrated simply her way of expressing kindness, or was there a spark to this new friendship suggesting something more? Though I only walked with her for one day, I felt as if I had known her much longer. After we talked for a while and finished our beers, I went upstairs and fell asleep immediately. Tomorrow the walk would be eleven miles to Villamayor de Monjardín.

Shortly after falling asleep I was awakened by a hand on my shoulder. I rolled over and saw Ella sitting on the empty bed next to mine.

"Hey, I'm sorry to wake you, but I must tell you that I cannot walk with you tomorrow."

Her words took a moment to register with my half-awake brain and I asked, "What? Why's that?"

"It's my mother; she wants me walking with her tomorrow in case she needs help. I need to be with her. I'm so sorry."

Ella's expression hinted at some sort of disagreement

between her and her mother. I understood the situation. The last thing Hanna probably wanted was for Ella to disappear with someone else. She was on the Camino to heal old wounds with her mother, and that was what she needed to do. We exchanged contact information and agreed to keep in touch. Ella apologized again and said, "I know we will see each other again on the Camino."

I felt empty inside after Ella went back to her room. I had only known her for a short time, but I already knew I would miss her company. Before starting the Camino, I read that every day on this journey had at least one lesson. Today was about letting people go, because as Tom said, "There is only your own pace."

Saying goodbye to people like Ella, Alma, and Beth was difficult, but they all taught me a lot about accepting help from others. The kindness they demonstrated to a complete stranger surprised me. Even with the difficulties of muscular dystrophy, I was always someone who focused on self-reliance, but seeing the happiness that people had from helping me made me realize it was okay to accept help. Showing compassion was just as important as accepting compassion. The next day was August 24, exactly one week since I left home, and already I felt like a different person. Sixty-seven miles were now behind me, and tomorrow I would finally face the Camino alone.

5

MY OWN PACE

I woke up at 5:30 a.m. and felt immediate sadness that I would not be walking with Ella. Without someone to help me and with the continuing heat wave, I decided to take a short five-mile day to Estella and not Villamayor de Monjardín. Around 6:00, I stepped outside into the darkness. After yesterday's wrong turn I knew the smart decision was to wait for daylight. There was no rush to be in Estella.

As I was waiting, Ella and her group came out. I hoped it would not look like I was waiting for them since Hanna obviously did not want me as a part of their group. After saying good morning, I explained I was waiting for more daylight. Hanna looked like she was ignoring me as I spoke, but I wished them a "Buen Camino," and they were gone. For a moment I wondered if I could just follow them, but I understood this was where we parted ways. I had to accept people coming and going in my journey.

By 6:45, it was light enough to start walking. The landscape was rural, but the view of the mountain Montejurra was visible to the south as a prominent bump in an otherwise flat dry landscape. Several pilgrims passed me on the dirt trail, but I kept to myself. This was the longest stretch I walked alone since beginning the Camino. Since St-Jean I had been continuously pushing my limits. Walking alone allowed me to realize that my long days had a lot to do with keeping up with who I was with. Now I could begin to put into practice Tom's wisdom about walking one's own pace. Relying on myself felt refreshing.

On an isolated downhill stretch of the trail, I suddenly heard several dogs barking from behind a grove of trees. I stopped for a moment and remembered all the stories I heard about wild dogs on the Camino. Suddenly I wished I was with other people again. A pack of four dogs came running towards me, barking more viciously now. I froze in place. They all stopped about four feet from me, barking and growling, with drool dripping from their mouths. They were all mutts with patchy hair and no collars around their necks.

I pointed my hiking pole at them, ready to hit and jab with all my strength if they attacked. The dogs were nipping and snarling at each other as if they were arguing over who would get me first. Slowly I inched toward the edge of the trail, not turning my back to them, and they continued to move towards me. My hand trembled as I swung my hiking pole in the air and yelled at the dogs. I wondered if I should throw my pack on the ground and run, hoping they would attack my pack instead. But my body would not allow me to run. I needed to stand my ground. Hopefully another pilgrim would approach on the trail and help me. This was something I could not handle on my own.

My heart continued to race as the dogs snarled at me. As I took a deep breath and expected the worst, another dog barked in the distance, and the pack of dogs ran in the direction of the bark. I sighed in relief as their barking faded away. After I continued walking, I saw a dog heading in my direction, but it paid little attention to me as it ran by. The dog looked like it was searching for the pack I had just encountered.

I was in the town of Estella before noon and spent most of the day napping in bed at my albergue. With little more than five miles completed today, I considered this a rest day. Having a break from the heat brought a much needed boost to my

My Own Pace

spirits. Early the next morning after leaving Estella, I heard footsteps approaching from behind and a familiar voice calling my name. I turned to see Florence.

"I thought for sure everyone from that first night in Orisson had passed me by now. How are you?" I asked, as she approached.

"Not well. My knees are hurting. Going uphill, going downhill, it all hurts. I bought some knee braces in Estella, but it still hurts. Do you want me to carry your pack?" Florence asked.

I laughed slightly, remembering what Hanna said about Florence always worrying about everyone but herself, and said, "Not in your condition. I'll be okay."

The terrain was steep but not enough for me to justify someone carrying my pack.

"Where is Ella?" she asked.

"She moved on ahead yesterday with her group."

"Oh, that's too bad, she seemed to really like you," Florence said.

"Yeah, well, that's how the Camino goes," I said.

The two of us stuck together for the rest of the day walking at a similar pace. While we were stopped at a café for lunch, Florence said, "I just keep thinking about you. If you can keep going, I can keep going with this knee pain."

"Well, I'm flattered, but I'm not Superman. If I'm in pain, I stop. You shouldn't push yourself too hard if it costs you an injury," I said.

"I know. I know. I just don't want to give up."

"Maybe you should take a short day too. I'm stopping in Villamayor just up the road."

"My pack was sent to Los Arcos, so I'm walking there today."

Los Arcos was an additional eight miles farther, and I knew Florence regretted her decision to send her pack so far ahead. Her desire to push as hard as she could was understandable.

My Own Pace

Watching everyone pass you on the trail can be heartbreaking, but you have to find your own pace.

By the time we got into Villamayor de Monjardín the heat was on the rise. My thoughts were on Florence and her eight mile stretch to Los Arcos, where there would be no towns or places to find water. With her pack in another town, there was no convincing her to stay. We sat on a bench outside a café as I decided on an albergue for the night and Florence filled up her water bottles. After exchanging contact information and a big hug, we parted ways. I had a feeling I would see her again but did not know if she would reach Santiago. As I went to bed that night at my albergue, I felt calm and relaxed about the coming days. I assumed I would have a series of uneventful days now that everyone I knew was ahead of me.

I was wrong. When I woke up the next morning, my journey took an unexpected turn. Around 5:00 a.m., I felt terrible itching all over my body. After further investigation, I found clusters of red welts on my arms, legs, neck, and back. Bed bugs! I had heard stories of albergues infested with them and hoped they were exaggerated, but the proof was on me. I got my gear together and quickly left the albergue.

Back on the trail, I needed to stop quite often to scratch the bites, and my feet began hurting before the sun was even up. The two short days were meant to relieve pain, but this was the earliest in the day my foot pain had ever started. My destination was the town of Torres del Río, about thirteen miles away. This seemed an incredible distance after walking only six miles yesterday. As the day went on, the bites became more inflamed, creating complete and utter misery. My hope was that the bugs were left in Villamayor and not in my pack waiting for their next chance to feast. This felt like something that could finally break me. After all I went through, would little insects be my downfall? I just wanted to be done with the Camino.

The albergue I stayed in that night had a swimming pool,

which I sat in for an hour to provide some relief from the itching. At dinner that night I asked some pilgrims if they knew anything about bed bugs, but no one had heard of it happening to anyone yet. All I could do was wash my clothes in a washing machine at the albergue. Tomorrow would be the test to see if I awoke with more bites.

That night I had dreams of bugs crawling on me, and the next morning proved this dream was reality. The amount of bites had doubled, and it felt like my entire body was on fire. My arms looked like I had chicken pox. The welts on my waistline and upper back were difficult to scratch with clothes on. I caught the Camino "plague" and needed to do something immediately, or it would ruin the rest of this journey.

After organizing my gear, I sat on a bench to tie my shoes and felt something crawling on my arm. I looked to find a round apple seed size bug scurrying across my skin. I quickly shooed it off and jumped to my feet, brushing off my shirt and pants. I could not find any more bugs, but I envisioned hundreds of them all over myself.

"Ugh, what am I going to do?" I thought.

As I spent the day walking to the city of Logroño, the biggest settlement I passed through since Pamplona, I felt incredibly lonely. Even though I walked off and on with a Brazilian woman from the albergue the night before, she spoke little English, and I began to wish I was with my group from my first few days again.

Washing my clothes again at the albergue in Logroño seemed to lessen the number of bites I woke up with the next morning, but still new bites persisted. Feeling numb to the itching by now, all I could do was trudge onward. The return to a rural landscape as I left the city that morning brought my mood up slightly, but dark clouds began to gather in the sky. As thunder began to rumble and a light drizzle of rain fell around me, I wanted to make it to the town of Navarrete quickly. After walking up a short hill and into an open field, the storm broke, and rain poured down. Lightning flashed all around me. I tried to get out of the field as quickly as possible. There were no structures or trees nearby to find cover, and I worried that my aluminum hiking pole made me a target. Up ahead was a hedgerow of bushes and weeds with a ditch to one side. I hurried over and took cover in the ditch as the storm intensified. While I was crouched low, I saw two girls rush over to the ditch on the other side of the trail and take shelter.

The storm raged on, and every lightning strike seemed closer than the last. Water dripping off the bushes slowly made me wet, and the soft soil I lay on was turning to mud. I was prepared to spend all day under the bushes if necessary, but after about thirty minutes the storm stopped as quickly as it started. I emerged from the ditch along with the two girls. They were both German and had long blond hair. We talked briefly about how frightened we were, but they moved ahead, and I continued to Navarrete.

Once in town, I ducked into a café just as a second storm came through and quickly passed. I debated spending the night in Navarrete instead of risking another storm on the way into Ventosa where I had planned on spending the night. An Italian couple I ate lunch with at the café urged me to stay, but the five miles to Ventosa was an easy two-hour walk. I wanted to save as much time as possible for rest days toward the end of the Camino, so I made the decision to move onward.

The slippery wet cobblestone streets through Navarrete circled around a small hilltop. There were few trail markers on the old faded stone buildings. This caused me to second guess if I was heading in the correct direction. The narrow street eventually led onto a paved road with cars parked along the sidewalk and several locals walking around. Even though many of the buildings looked abandoned and eerie, everyone in town seemed friendly and had a comfortable pep in their pace. I put my pack down on a bench and checked my guidebook to see if I was on the right road. Everything looked in order. Just as I was putting my pack back on, I saw a woman in her mid-sixties with a large backpack and short grey hair stop and look at her map. Clearly I was not the only pilgrim confused by the winding streets.

As I looked over at her, she asked in a southern American accent, "Do you know if this is the way?"

"I think so," I replied, as she walked over to me.

"I think so too," she said, as she tucked her map into a side pocket of her pack.

"Where are you from?" we both asked each other at the same moment and laughed.

The woman's name was Eleanor, and she was from Texas. She talked in a slow, nervous tone suggesting an apprehension in talking to strangers. I was the first American she met in several days, which always caused a natural gravitation toward another. Eleanor recently retired from a long career as a school teacher and was finally taking some time to see the world.

"I hope it's alright if I walk with you since I walk so slowly," Eleanor said.

I told her I did not mind her pace, and that I had muscular dystrophy and walked slowly as well. After briefly explaining how the condition affected me, Eleanor said, "I just can't believe you came out here and made it this far with your condition. You are such an inspiration to me. I hope you won't take that the wrong way."

As we continued, the sounds of thunder dissipated, and the dark clouds blew away revealing a bright sun and a landscape dominated by perfect rows of grapevines in every direction. Eleanor and I both stopped to remove our rain gear. I knew I made the right decision to leave Navarrete. The Camino left the main road a few minutes out of town and led down a dirt trail that was completely saturated from the rain. After only a few steps, our shoes became caked in mud, adding extra effort to each step.

The lonely feelings I felt the first half of the day began to fade as Eleanor's mother-like personality and genuine concern put me at ease. In our conversation, Eleanor talked about the training she did for the Camino and how many people thought she was crazy for attempting this journey, but the support from her husband was her biggest motivation. She told a story about her husband following her in his truck as she walked down country roads in Texas while training. Walking alone with a bulky backpack on the Camino sometimes made her feel vulnerable, so she often imagined her husband behind her in his truck.

Eleanor told me how much I reminded her of her son who was a world traveler and currently lived in India. She was planning to visit him after she finished the Camino. When we finally reached Ventosa, Eleanor said, "I have enjoyed walking with you so much and want to stop here with you, but being with you has given me so much inspiration that I am going to keep walking to Nájera. You have made me feel so good. I feel like I have been walking with my son."

After taking down my name, Eleanor said she would find me on Facebook. Maybe I would see her again, or maybe she would fade away like so many others. Every so often, you meet someone whose image and voice remain ingrained in your mind. Eleanor was one of those people, proving that the character of an individual, not the amount of time spent with them, serves as the primary criteria for leaving an impression.

I was the first pilgrim to check into the albergue in Ventosa that afternoon. After taking a short nap, a group of three Australians checked into my room. One of them was a guy named Rob who I met briefly on the trail the day before. He asked me, "How are you feeling? You looked like you were having some trouble the last time I saw you."

"Yeah, I'm alright. I have muscular dystrophy, so I have trouble walking up hills," I said.

"Oh, so that's just the way you walk?"

My Own Pace

"Yeah."

"That's great that you're still able to walk the Camino," Rob said.

While Rob and I were talking, the last two people assigned to our room walked through the door, who proved to be familiar faces. Connor and his wife, Evelyn, were the American couple from Florida whom I met in Uterga, where I met Ella and parted ways with Beth and Alma. Connor's thick grey hair and Evelyn's thick framed glasses were not easy to forget. Evelyn overheard my conversation with Rob and asked, "What's wrong with you?"

"I have muscular dystrophy. So it's made things a bit difficult."

"I would have never known. Congrats for making it this far," Connor said.

Everyone mostly kept to themselves that evening, but it was nice to finally be among familiar pilgrims again. I slept well that night, despite Connor's snoring that kept me up for a couple hours. I did not have any new bed bug bites the next morning, so my spirits were feeling a little higher than usual. Hopefully washing my clothes again the night before finally helped.

After grabbing a quick breakfast from a café down the street from the albergue, I headed down a dirt road out of Ventosa, but a dense fog blocked the view more than a few feet ahead. Just past a winery, the road split, and there were no trail markers. I turned around to see if I missed a yellow arrow, and the figure of a petite woman emerged from the fog. She was a pilgrim I had seen on the trail several times in the past few days. Her unique look made her hard to forget. Over her curly black hair she wore a brown floppy fedora with a purple flower on the side. She wore a loose fitting green shirt, an orange dress with a multicolored pattern, and an old worn out pair of sneakers. The tall walking stick she carried had feathers tied around the top, and her dirty red hiking backpack had a sleeping pad tied on the top, making her look like an ancient pilgrim from the Middle Ages.

The woman smiled as she approached, and I asked, "This is the way, right?"

"Yes. We can walk together if you want. It is okay," she replied in a French accent.

Her name was Naomi, and she was thirty-eight years old but appeared to be in her late twenties. The youthful look came from her beaming smile and high cheekbones, but looking more closely revealed a slightly weathered appearance. She lived and worked on a farm in southern France with her husband and young son. I learned she had little money and spent most of her nights on the Camino sleeping outside. Naomi described herself as being on a pilgrimage of self-growth.

The trail made its way through farmland and became very hilly and rocky. Part of the trail was washed out and muddy from yesterday's rain. Little gullies were carved out of the thick clay exposing jagged rocks. I told Naomi I had muscular dystrophy, so she would understand why I was having so much difficulty. I expected her to move ahead, but to my surprise she walked slowly and offered her hand in places where I had to take wide steps from rock to rock. I thanked her for helping, and she said, "Every day is a gift, and the people we meet throughout the day are a part of that gift."

As the trail leveled out and the fog cleared, Naomi began singing a song in French. Her voice was enchanting as rays of sunlight lit up the trail and made the surroundings glow. She said she loved to sing every morning because it helped to clear her mind. We discovered we shared a liking of the American band Sublime, so she started singing the song, "What I Got." After she sang the first verse, I chimed in with the second verse, until we were both belting out the chorus at the top of our lungs.

After we finished the song we were laughing just as hard

as we were singing. We were completely removed from any obligations besides walking, and it felt nice to let loose and sing at the top of my lungs. Even though she had little money, she was the happiest person I had met on the Camino. There was never a moment she was not smiling. Every time we passed a flower or heard an interesting bird sing, she pointed it out and said how beautiful it was, and whenever another pilgrim passed us, she waved to them and said, "Hola," in a cheerful voice. The gravel trail eventually led us through a vineyard with large, juicy purple grapes hanging from the vines. Naomi hurried over and picked a large clump, handed me half, and we both ate our fill.

"Are we allowed to eat these grapes?" I asked.

"No, you just cannot get caught," she said, with a chuckle.

We continued into the town of Nájera, which was the midway point of my twelve miles to Azofra. Nájera appeared after we passed under a highway near a construction site, and we followed a paved road out of the countryside and onto a sidewalk. Though the town was small, along the main road were several large apartment complexes with shops and stores on the ground floors. We stopped in a café for rest midway through the town. The décor of the café was of higher class than our attire, with a shiny wooden bar and tables with white tablecloths.

I bought a muffin and offered to buy Naomi something, but she said she had enough for a glass of wine, and that was all she wanted. She opened a small wallet and counted out a few coins. The only thing she asked from me was to use my cell phone to send a text message to her family to let them know she was safe. Feeling happy to offer her anything I could, I gladly handed her my phone. Several people in the café were wearing suits and ties, so not wanting to disturb the atmosphere, I picked a table in the corner away from the bar. While we were resting, all my bug bites started itching. Naomi had several noticeable bites on her arms too, though I did not comment since I knew how skeevy it felt to have your infestation known to everyone.

After our rest, we continued through the bustling streets of Nájera. Naomi asked if we could stop in a church at the edge of town, and I agreed. The building did not resemble a church from the outside. It was squeezed between two buildings in a series of shops and apartments, and all that was visible was a stone wall with an arched doorway, and two green and blue stained glass windows on the second level. I walked across the marble floor and sat in a pew. Naomi knelt down and prayed in front of a sparkling gold and silver altar with a statue of the Virgin Mary holding baby Jesus.

My late grandmother was a deeply religious Catholic, and I wondered what she would have thought if she could see me now. She would have been happy to see me on a pilgrimage to the tomb of Saint James but probably sad to know I did not practice that faith anymore. After Naomi finished praying, she quietly stood up and we continued on.

"Are you Catholic?" Naomi asked, as we began walking.

"No, I'm not. I don't really have a faith."

"Are you an atheist?" she asked.

"I don't know. I usually just call myself agnostic."

"I am not a Catholic either, but I do believe in God."

"I do believe in something. I just don't know what it is."

"There are more ways to believe in God than there are people on Earth, and I am on the Camino to discover my own way," Naomi said.

"God is more of an internal concept for me. I think people are inherently good and experience both heaven and hell within their life. So people use their own judgments to navigate the journey," I responded.

"No one can tell anyone if they are right or wrong. You do not have to believe in God to believe in God. When someone helps someone in need, that is God. When someone shows love for a stranger, that is God. When someone chooses the path of wisdom, that is God. And you don't have to believe in God to see those kinds of things. There is something good we can learn from all people and ideas."

I thought about what Naomi said and about what God meant to me. My mother is Catholic, and my father is Baptist. I was raised Catholic and received all my sacraments but never believed in any of it. Ideas rooted in facts and tangible ideas were how I gained an understanding of the world. I never felt pressured by my parents to continue following a tradition I did not believe and left Catholicism when I was a teenager. There was a time in my life where I tried to become a Christian, or at least pondered the idea. During my senior year of high school, I started attending a youth group at a Baptist church in my town with some friends. I really tried to identify with Christianity but just could not relate to anything they said. Most ideas relating to organized religion seemed too complex. Naomi's explanation made more sense to me.

Leaving Nájera, the trail led us over the shallow fast-moving Najerilla River. Many colorful rocks were visible through the clear water from atop the cobblestone bridge. The small section of town on the other side of the river backed up to a treeless hillside. Some vegetation grew on top of the hill, but the mostly bare rock reminded me of the American Southwest with its sandstone color. The trail turned onto a paved road around the hill past some old abandoned buildings, until we found ourselves again on a dirt trail through the countryside. Another hill after town, along with the still present humidity, slowed me down and left me huffing for breath. Naomi took the water bottle out of the side pocket of my pack for me, and I took a slow swig. While I was catching my breath, Naomi put her hand on my shoulder like a caring friend and said, "Your strength is wisdom."

I was not sure exactly what that statement meant, but I smiled and said, "Thanks." Maybe Naomi meant she was gaining wisdom by seeing me struggle, or maybe she meant my strength to keep moving came from a deeply rooted drive within myself. Regardless of what she meant, I was using every ounce of strength I had, and that was teaching me wisdom.

An hour outside of Azofra, Naomi laid down her sleeping pad near a dirt crossroads, and we both sat for a rest. The grass was still wet from yesterday's rain. To the left of the road was another vineyard with thick vines, and on the right was a freshly plowed field. Naomi offered to share an apple, but I declined because she needed it more than me. I offered her a granola bar, but she said an apple was enough. She looked skinny and malnourished from living off what she could find. I wondered why she refused to accept anything from me. Sitting close to Naomi, I caught a whiff of her dirty clothes, and I doubted she had a change of clothes in her pack.

As we rested, she hummed a song and tore a piece of cloth off of her frayed dress. She removed her shoe and wrapped the cloth around her foot where a blister was forming. I offered her a bandage from my pack, but she declined, saying, "No, this works better. I did this on my other foot and it helped."

I saw a pilgrim approaching from up the road and recognized it was Rob from my room the night before.

"Hey Bryan! We're almost at Azofra, I reckon?" he asked, as he passed.

"I think so," I responded, happy to see a familiar face, "You're still stopping there for the night?"

"Yeah, I'll see you up there," he said, as he continued on, and we followed a few minutes after.

As the trail turned from dirt to a paved road and the red roofs of Azofra appeared on the horizon, Naomi took out a shaker, started making a rhythm, and sang a reggae song. As we walked and she sang, an Australian girl, named Sarah, from Rob's group, came up from behind and listened. I nodded hello to her, but we both remained silent as Naomi continued singing. Something about Naomi's voice and demeanor were so enchanting that she seemed to captivate anyone who crossed her path.

We reached the quaint streets of Azofra around noon. The faded stone buildings and adobe homes with chipped yellow and tan paint had a calming ambiance. An old woman in a blue dress was sweeping dust off her front porch into the narrow cement street. We walked until we found Rob in the town center waiting for Sarah. The albergue opened at 1:00, so we had some time to relax. Rob sat on a fountain in the shape of an armchair with two steps at its base and water flowing from four small pipes into a long narrow grate. A light fixture stuck out of the top, and a sign stated the water was not potable. Naomi sat by the side of the fountain, removed her sneakers and washed her legs and arms. She looked peaceful and elegant despite her tattered clothes. Naomi decided she would not stop in Azofra but would continue on to find somewhere to sleep outside. After exchanging contact information, Naomi said, "Au revoir Monsieur Bryan, until we meet again," and walked away down the road. I did not know it then, but I would not cross paths with her again.

I was one of the first to arrive at the albergue. The building was narrow and in an L-shape with three floors. A wooden fence formed a courtyard area between the two wings of the building. I was assigned a bed on the first floor in one of the many jail-cell-size rooms each with two beds. The room had a small one-person deck with a view of the countryside. Rows of grapevines stretched out as far as I could see with a backdrop of rolling tree-covered hills. Rob came in a few minutes later and put his pack on the other bed.

After we settled in he asked, "Who was the lady you were walking with today? She looked like a real pilgrim."

"Yeah, her name is Naomi. She hardly has any money, and she sleeps outside, yet she's still walking the Camino," I said.

Rob nodded, taking in the information. I could tell he was

as impressed by Naomi as I had been. "That's pretty wild. She's on a whole other level than pilgrims like us. Amazing."

Rob and I talked for a while about how far we had come, and the struggles we each faced over the past few days. Rob drained a huge blister on his toe as we talked. My feet were sore, but somehow I still managed to avoid blisters. I did have a few warm, red spots on my toes that I covered with strips of moleskin as a precaution.

Connor and Evelyn were in the room on the other side. They both stopped by our room to say hello later in the afternoon and asked how our day was, awaking Rob and me from our naps. After they left, Rob shared with me information he heard about them. This was Connor and Evelyn's fourth time walking the Camino. Their first Camino was in 2014 after their daughter, and only child, passed away suddenly at the age of nineteen. Walking the Camino was their way of grieving. I noticed that Connor seemed to take a strong interest in Rob and me. I wondered if this had to do with the fact that his daughter would have been around the same age of us if she were still alive.

Later in the evening I went to a restaurant in town for dinner. I ordered chicken and spaghetti with meat sauce. It tasted bland and dry, but it left me feeling stuffed, and I developed a slight stomach ache. I spent the rest of the night resting at the albergue. My stomach was still sore a few hours later, and I began to wonder if it was because I ate too much or if I was getting sick. Rob and his group cooked their own dinner of pasta in the albergue kitchen. They offered me some, and even though I wanted to join them, the idea of more food made my stomach hurt even more. I went to sleep soon after and hoped for a better morning.

I awoke at 3:00 a.m. and vomited all over my bed and the floor. My nose and throat burned as I spat out fluids everywhere. I rushed to the bathroom down the hall, burst open a stall and vomited again into the toilet. My body was shaking and sweating as I hunched over the toilet with my chin leaning on the cold white ceramic. Vomit continued to pour from my mouth until I found myself on the floor dry-heaving as the sounds echoed down the hallway. Memories flashed into my mind of being a sick child and having my mother take care of me. Now I was thousands of miles away from home, alone in a strange place. I knew my sickness was from last night's dinner. After feeling some relief, I stuck my head under the faucet and rinsed my mouth out. My reflection in the rusty mirror showed a pale face with heavy bloodshot eyes.

"I wanna go home," I said out loud.

I rinsed my mouth again and grabbed a roll of toilet paper and went back to the room to clean up the vomit. As I turned the lights on, Rob rolled over to see me cleaning the mess.

"Are you alright man?"

"Yeah, I got sick and threw up."

"Do you need help with anything?"

"Nah, I should be okay, but thanks."

"Alright, let me know if you need anything," he said, as he went back to sleep.

While cleaning the floor, I found new bed bug bites on my arms. They are easy to distinguish because they are usually in a cluster of several bites in a row. This moment felt like the lowest point of my Camino. All I wanted to do was go home. Perhaps I could catch a bus to Santiago and get a new flight home. Maybe the smart people were those who avoided struggle instead of deliberately seeking it out. I was tired of bed bugs, tired of walking, tired of the heat, tired of pain, and tired of eating strange food. Was one hundred twenty miles where this journey ended? I tried to go back to sleep but instead tossed and turned for several hours.

At 5:30 a.m., I decided to leave Azofra and start walking. I just wanted to run far away from the place that got me sick and all my negative thoughts about giving up on the Camino. Rob was still asleep as I left. Hoping my stomach was clean of whatever I ate, I quickly munched on a granola bar to replenish the lost energy. Against what I knew was the wrong decision, I walked thirteen miles to the town of Grañón. The little food in my stomach was thrown up within the first mile, and I continued to vomit along the trail into the afternoon. By the time my destination appeared on the horizon I felt shaky and clammy and wanted to just collapse into a bed.

When I found the albergue, which was in a large stone church, I noticed a pharmacy across the street and stopped there to buy medicine. I opened the door and was hit by a welcomed blast of cool air. I said hello to a blond-haired woman behind the counter dressed in white scrubs. Not realizing there was a step down inside the doorway, I lost my balance and fell to my knees.

"Ay Dios mío!" the pharmacist yelled as she rushed over and tried to help me to my feet before I could collect myself. I had to stop her from pulling me up so I could take my pack off and push myself up from the ground.

"I'm fine," I said, as I got to my feet.

"What is wrong?" the pharmacist asked, and looked down at my legs.

"I didn't realize there was a step there, but it's my stomach, I think I have food poisoning. Do you have any medicine?" I asked, as she walked back behind the counter.

I explained my symptoms, and she handed me two bottles of electrolyte drink and a box of antibacterial tablets to mix into water.

"Drink these two bottles throughout the course of today and tomorrow and take one tablet a day until you finish the box," she said, as she rang me up at the register.

I thanked her and she asked where I walked from that day. When I said Azofra her expression changed to that of an angry mother whose child spoiled his appetite for dinner.

"No! No! No! No! You don't do that! You rest. Where are you staying?"

76

My Own Pace

"The church across the street."

"Rest there today and tomorrow. They will take good care of you. You need to flush out your system."

I thanked her again, paid, and was about to leave when she glanced at the bed bug bites on my arm and asked, "What is this?"

"Oh, I got some bed bug bites. I'll be alright though," I said, not wanting to openly advertise I was potentially infested with bugs.

"Oh no! Wash clothes again," she said.

"Yeah, but they are old bites, so I'm alright now."

She gave me a half convinced smile and handed me a pack of anti-itch wipes she had on the counter and said, "Use this."

I thanked her and went across the street to the church. The front double wooden doors were locked, so I walked around the back to a small grassy square with neatly trimmed shrubs around the perimeter. Several trees in the square cast shadows on the side of the church, providing refreshing shade in the increasing heat of the day. A young stocky man with a balding head exited an open doorway of the church carrying a bucket and mop. He placed the cleaning supplies against the side of the building and looked up at me. Understanding I was a pilgrim, he welcomed me inside and spoke a few words of Spanish I did not understand. After explaining I only spoke English, we shook hands, and he introduced himself as John. He looked at the bag of items I purchased at the pharmacy as I stepped into a dark entry room.

"This is medicine I bought. I'm sick. I need to stay here tonight and take a rest day here tomorrow as well."

John gave me a confused look and said, "Puedes venir conmigo," and ushered me inside.

I followed him up a winding, stone staircase to the third floor that had my legs feeling stiff by the time I reached the top. There was another gentleman about my age with a stern

77

expression, neatly combed black hair, wearing a black button-up shirt, who greeted me and introduced himself as Fernando. He and John began speaking to each other in Spanish. The room had a kitchen area, dining table, and several couches and chairs. Above the room was a loft with several sleeping mats on the floor. Open-framed windows overlooked the grassy square and allowed the room to fill with natural light.

"Ah, you will rest here with us then," Fernando said firmly, after John finished speaking with him.

Suddenly the pharmacist from across the street entered the room with a look of high energy. What felt like a relaxing situation suddenly became stressful. She started speaking to Fernando and John, explaining that I was sick, and she pointed to the bites on my arms. I should have known. Fernando and John's demeanor changed when bed bugs were mentioned.

"You will wash your clothes in the washing machine here, but first you must put your stuff downstairs."

The pharmacist wished me well, and I thanked her for her help. She put her hand on my shoulder and gave me a heartfelt smile. Fernando immediately directed me downstairs to my room. This was an overflow room for when the loft was filled. The room had stone walls, a worn hardwood floor, and two large open frame windows. I knew they were putting me down here because of my bed bugs, which was the main reason I did not want to broadcast it in the first place. Their fears were understandable, as I would not wish the misery of bed bugs on anyone.

Fernando watched as I sat down on one of several brown sleeping mats and took everything out of my pack. I put all of my clothes in my sleeping bag sack and Fernando asked, "Are you almost ready to wash your things?"

Feeling annoyed by him pressuring me to wash everything, I paused before saying, "Yeah, I'm ready."

"What about the clothes you are wearing?"

"I washed all my clothes yesterday, so they are clean," I

My Own Pace

said, not wanting to separate myself from all of my belongings at once.

"Also you need to put your shoes by the door. Those are the rules," he said.

After I put my clothes in the albergue's washing machine, I went back to my room and Fernando followed me inside, He asked, "So how are you feeling now?"

"Much better," I said.

"The pharmacist gave you some medicine?" Fernando asked.

"Yes, I am going to start drinking it now," I said.

"Good, you should start now," he said, as he watched me open the bottle of electrolyte fluid.

"I'll be fine now," I said, looking up from the open bottle.

Fernando paused for a moment and then said, "Okay I will leave you now. I do not think you will throw up again," as he left the room and closed the door behind him.

I breathed a sigh of relief after he left. I dropped one of the anti-bacterial tablets in the drink and took a few sips, but after a few minutes my stomach began to rumble again. I hurried out of the room and to the bathroom next door. John was coming down the steps, and he asked me in broken English, "You okay?"

I tried to answer him, but I was about to vomit. With one hand over my mouth, I burst into the bathroom just as the vomit sprayed out into the sink.

I heard John hurrying up the steps yelling, "Fernando! Fernando! Doctor! Doctor!"

The bathroom smelled of vomit scented with the fruity electrolyte drink. I took a handful of toilet paper and wiped the sink and mirror that was splattered with debris. After I finished, I came out of the bathroom to find Fernando waiting outside. John stood closely behind him.

"We are going to call a doctor for you," Fernando said, as

My Own Pace

I walked back to my sleeping mat. John stood in the doorway as Fernando followed me.

"No, that will not be necessary," I said.

"You are sick, and you need a doctor."

"No, it's just simple food poisoning. I am fine without a doctor," I snapped back to him.

Fernando folded his arms and said in an Orwellian manner, "You are under our care now, and we will decide what is best for you."

I wanted to grab my stuff and hightail it out of there, but my clothes were still in the wash. I was trapped. Perhaps I should have remained in Azofra another night.

"Please do not call a doctor. I do not have money for a doctor," I said.

"No, you do not listen. We will decide what we do for you. Perhaps we will need to call an ambulance if the doctor cannot come," Fernando said.

"Look," I said, becoming more firm. "I just have an upset stomach. I'm not dying. I'm alright."

"Well, we will be responsible if you become more ill. We cannot allow this."

"Okay, how about this, if I throw up again you can call a doctor."

He seemed unsure of my response and thought for a moment, put his hand to his chin, and stroked his non-existent facial hair.

"But if you throw up again, we will have no choice but to call a doctor," he said, pointing his finger like he had authority over me.

"Okay, whatever," I said, as I thought about how I would not get caught when I threw up again.

"What year were you born?" he asked.

"1993."

"What month is your birthday?" he asked.

Wondering why he was asking, I slowly said, "July."

My Own Pace

"Ah, so you are older than me. I was born in December 1993."

"Okay," I said, unsure of his reasoning.

"We will still call a doctor if you throw up again."

"Alright, fine,' I said, as I rolled my eyes.

I spent the rest of the day resting, drinking my electrolyte drink, and concentrating on not throwing up. I spoke briefly with several pilgrims who were put into my room but mostly kept to myself. At dinner I was served plain rice to slowly reintroduce solid food into my stomach. That evening when I lay down to sleep, feeling that my stomach had completely returned to normal, I felt a rumbling in my large intestine. Jumping up from my mat, I hurried to the bathroom. My pants were hardly pulled down and my body was not fully positioned over the toilet when the destruction came. With an explosive force, a blast of diarrhea came out and splattered all over the toilet. The sounds of my expulsion echoed throughout the single person bathroom and probably throughout the albergue. I sat on the toilet leaning forward and shaking with internal discomfort as a few more rounds of liquid poured out of me. Maybe Fernando was right about seeing a doctor. All of the fluids I was losing would surely dehydrate me if this continued.

After feeling relieved, I turned to the mess covering the toilet, floor, and several spots on the wall. I unwound handfuls of toilet paper and began cleaning. The sight and smell made me gag and nearly vomit the little food I managed to keep down. This was probably now the most unsanitary bathroom in all of Spain. If I asked Fernando for cleaning supplies, he would know the seriousness of my illness and call a doctor. I cleaned the bathroom until there were no visible signs of what transpired. I hoped this ordeal was over and my body was finally cleansed, but these new struggles were only just beginning.

6

ULTREIA

Waking up the next morning, I felt another rumble in my bowels and rushed to the bathroom, confirming that my troubles would continue into another day. Luckily, the volunteer staff at the albergue changed that morning, so I was no longer under the overly watchful eyes of Fernando as I continued to run to the bathroom every half hour. Throughout the day I exchanged a few text messages with Beth. She explained how Alma had developed tendonitis in her feet and stopped walking in Burgos, while Beth continued into the Meseta on bike to make up for lost time. When I arrived in Burgos in three days, I planned to see Alma if she was still there. I also learned that Florence's knee problem forced her to end her Camino, and she would also be resting in Burgos when I arrived. Ella sent me a message that day asking how I was doing. Her group was now a two day's walk ahead of me, so I would not be catching up with her anytime soon. If not for my rest day, I might have been able to see her in Burgos too. Tomorrow I would be leaving Grañón whether I was sick or well.

The next morning brought more diarrhea. When I looked in the toilet I saw solid bits of everything I ate for dinner the evening before. Everything I ate was flowing directly out of me. I wondered how many calories I gained from what I ate, and if I should continue on or take another rest day. This could go on for a week, and I did not have a week to sit around. For the previous fourteen days and one hundred thirty-six miles the Camino provided, so I knew things would somehow work out. Despite my illness, one positive aspect of the morning was that there were no new bed bug bites. Today was September 1, and a new month felt like a good day to regroup and keep moving.

The walk out of Grañón in the dark through the farmland was peaceful and quiet. Just beyond town was a slight hill, but I made sure to take it slow and not push myself too hard. A half mile into my day, I turned around to see the last glimpse of Grañón. The steeple of the church rose high above the town in front of a brilliant orange sunrise. The rolling hills covered by wheat fields appeared a golden color as light illuminated them. Even though I was happy to be on the move, I was leaving behind the security of having a place to rest and not worry about when my next round of diarrhea would come.

The beautiful view was met by the stark contrast of a familiar rumbling in my intestines. The next town was a mile away, but I knew I could be back in Grañón in half that distance. Reluctantly moving forward, I came across a large kiosk and sign showing a map of the Camino through the province of Castile y León. I looked around and saw there were no other pilgrims anywhere in sight. This was where I would release the load. I walked around the other side of the sign, put my pack on the ground, pulled down my pants and squatted. Feeling the wind on my bare skin and hearing the sound of matter hitting the gravelly soil beneath me was degrading to say the least. When I imagined the beauty and romance of walking across Spain, this was not what I envisioned. With no shovel to bury the mess, I left the scene, hoping no one would stumble upon the horrific surprise.

Luckily the rest of my walk for the day did not have any moments where I needed to find privacy on the side of the trail. I chose not to eat much throughout the day, so my stomach was growling with hunger by the time I reached my destination for the day in Tostanos. That evening at a restaurant next to my albergue. I ordered the three course meal of chicken with salad, vegetable soup, and ice cream for dessert. I do not know if the food was really that good or if I was just really hungry from hardly eating all day, but it tasted amazing. The soup was thick with large chunks of potatoes, carrots, long noodles, and spinach. The chicken was tender and pulled right off the bones. Midway through the bliss of eating, I felt a rumble in my large intestine. I made a dash to the café bathroom next to my table, but the door seemed locked, so I stood to wait for whoever was in there to come out. After a minute of standing, no one came out. Should I knock after I already tried the handle? I did not want to pester whoever might be in there. Should I keep waiting? Maybe the door was locked. I wanted to avoid another conversation with someone who did not speak English. Being in a foreign country made these moments more stressful than they should be. I decided to finish my meal and get back to the albergue to use that bathroom, unless the bathroom here opened before then.

Moments after sitting down, I felt an uncontrollable release of gas, and a rush of warm fluid beneath me. I needed to get back to my room immediately. I called the woman behind the counter over to pay, have the rest of my meal boxed, and take my ice-cream cone to go. But what was I going to do about the mess under me? I could not just leave it there. While the woman took my plate and handed me my bill, I asked her if the bathroom was locked since no one came out yet. She said no, and ushered me to follow her to check on the door. I was reluctant to stand up because I knew some of the customers would see a large brown spot on my pants and the mess on the seat. When I stood up, I glanced down, and pushed my chair in with horror. How was I going to clean this up? As I walked to the bathroom, my back turned to a group of five old men who were eating and talking loudly. The chatter became quieter as I walked by. Thoughts flooded into my mind of when I wet my pants in kindergarten, and the whole class laughed at me. I am a grown adult, not a five-year-old. These kinds of things do not happen. The woman gave the bathroom door a hard push, and it opened with a squeak, revealing it was only stuck. I rushed inside to clean myself.

With my pockets loaded with toilet paper to discreetly clean the seat, I slowly opened the door. The five men were completely silent and looking at me as I passed by again with my head down. At least I would never have to see them again. The hostess handed me my boxed meal and ice cream cone as I sat down. I felt the matter beneath me slush and move as I pulled in my seat. While I tried to enjoy my dessert, I pondered how I would clean this mess. Once I finished my ice cream, I took the toilet paper out of my pocket and stood up. With a few wipes, I collected the diarrhea and slid the wad of paper into my pocket. For whoever sat in that chair after me, I sincerely apologize.

Once back in the albergue, I washed all of my dirty clothes in the sink and took a shower. I wished the shower could have washed away the embarrassment I felt, but tomorrow this place, like everywhere else, would be another memory for better or worse.

The next day the Camino began to lead to higher elevations after several days of relatively flat ground. An area known as the Orca Hills began the start of the plateau which was to eventually become the Meseta after Burgos. I was looking forward to the Meseta, since the long stretch of flat land would allow my body to rest before the last series of mountains before Santiago.

The three-mile climb to the top of the Orca Hills was much harder than I anticipated. The initial section was narrow with several washed out portions littered with loose rocks. Dense trees walled each side of the trail as I moved away from the scattered buildings on the outskirts of Villafranca. A wave of pilgrims leaving town began their ascent up the hill at the same time, and I had to keep stopping to let people pass. The feeling that I was a burden or people were judging me on how I walked weighed heavily on my mind even though no one commented. I should have been familiar with this feeling by now, but it still saddened me.

On a relatively level portion, midway up the hill, I came to a log on the side of the trail. I sat down to rest my muscles and let the influx of pilgrims pass by. My skin was starting to feel sticky as the day's heat intensified, so I took a few big swigs of water. As the pilgrims walked by, I began to think about how these strangers had no idea how difficult the hill was for me. When I was just sitting and drinking water, I was no different than any other pilgrim. Then the thought crossed my mind that I had no idea how difficult these pilgrims' lives might be. I could look at anyone and think, "Man, I wish I had their muscles," and someone could look at me and think, "I wish I was as happy as him. I wish I could live a life where I did not have to bury my own child, or I wish I came from a home where people worried about me." The more I thought about how everyone had their own struggles, the more I was reminded that I was the same as everyone else. Like Tom said, we are all just moving at "our own pace" and living life the best that we can. The reason I felt down about other pilgrims passing me was because I was trying to be like them. We can only strive to be ourselves.

A few minutes after I started walking again, I met a tall older man with receding grey hair and green eyes. I said hello and he greeted me back in what sounded like an American accent.

"Are you hurt? You look like you're having a bit of an issue moving," he asked, in a warm friendly voice.

I explained my situation, and he introduced himself as George, a recently retired therapist from Canada. As we talked he said, "It's funny how I was a therapist my whole life and always told people how to deal with their problems, but it wasn't until I came on the Camino and faced the biggest struggle of my life that I realized I'm the one who needs help!"

"I guess there's no better place to realize that than here on the Camino," I said.

"I can't even imagine how much harder it is for you. You're an inspiration coming out here with muscular dystrophy," he said.

"I'm just doing the best I can," I continued.

"Well, you are my therapy for the day."

I was slightly tired of people calling me an inspiration. The novelty of the good feeling I had when people told me how amazing it was for me to be walking the Camino was no longer there. After having so many people flow in and out of my journey, I saw that everyone had their own difficulties. Having muscular dystrophy no longer defined me as an individual on this journey. A disability only defines who we are if we allow it to. As I continued talking to George, my annoyance began to fade as the conversation became deeper.

"I found a book at an albergue a few days ago, called *Man's Search for Meaning*, by Holocaust survivor Viktor Frankl. Just finished it yesterday evening. I was going to leave it on the side of the trail for someone else, but you might like it. It really helped me," George said.

"Oh, thanks. That would be nice. I didn't bring any books with me."

"I was just thinking about how he explained that freedom is one thing that can never be taken from someone. Everyone has the freedom to control the way they look at the circumstances they are in."

"Yeah, that's true, especially on the Camino. Nothing about this is inherently fun, in the traditional sense of the word, but our mindsets make it worthwhile, I guess."

"Yes, exactly. Circumstance means nothing in our ability to find meaning in our lives."

Before George finally passed me, he reached into his pack

and handed me an old worn book with frayed pages and said, "Just promise me when you finish it, you leave it for someone else to read. There's a powerful message in this book."

Later that morning, the trail leveled out for a while before heading downhill into a small valley with a bridge over a stream. The elevation change felt relaxing after the climb, but the closer I got to the bridge, the steeper the other side of the valley looked. On the other side of the bridge, a muscular man with dark hair and a short trimmed beard joined me. After the usual pilgrim introductions, he described himself as a twenty-six-year-old Spaniard from Valencia named Roberto. He spoke perfect English and seemed like good company, but with the approaching climb, I expected him to move ahead. A few feet up the hill, he noticed my sudden change in pace, so I explained my condition.

"Do you want me to help pull you up the hill?"

"No, that's alright," I said.

He stopped and looked at me as I inched up the hill and said, "How about I carry you on my back?"

I laughed out loud, since he was carrying his own heavy pack and could not possibly carry me. I hardly had the time to answer when he took off his pack and squatted on the ground for me to get on his back. The thought of this seemed ridiculous. How was an absolute stranger offering me a ride on his back?

"What about my pack?" I said, as I lifted the strap off my shoulder for a moment, indicating there was no way he could carry me and my pack.

"Leave it here, and I'll walk back down the hill for it."

Roberto was squatting on the ground waiting for me to climb on, and I could not think of a single reason to say no. If this interaction happened on my first day, I would have turned around and stopped walking. This kindness would seem completely idiotic to someone who had never been in an environment like the Camino. With complete disregard to whatever was socially normal, I climbed onto Roberto's back and gripped his shoulders tightly as he grabbed my legs, stood up, and marched up the hill.

"What is happening right now?" I thought to myself as he carried me about a hundred feet up the hill. Something deep within my psyche changed for me to accept this help. This was kindness to a degree I had never witnessed. With others who assisted me, a friendship had developed to some extent before most of their help began. What I was experiencing now was someone's willingness to help with no regard to what I had to offer in return. At the top of the hill, Roberto knelt down, and I plopped down on my feet.

"Gee, thanks," I said, as Roberto immediately hurried down the hill to grab both of our packs and lugged them back up. I reached out to grab my pack, and he disregarded my arm and placed the pack on my shoulders.

"You're an incredible human being," I said.

"No, you are the incredible human being. I am just being what every human being should be."

"Where are you walking to today?" I asked, after a few moments in silence, as I tried to process his act of kindness.

"Burgos. You?'

"Wow, I won't be there till tomorrow. I'm walking to Agés."

With his long distance left to walk for the day, I knew I would not be with him much longer. In a few minutes, he wished me well, and like many of the others I encountered, I never saw him again.

The physically challenging day left me exhausted by the time I arrived at my albergue in Agés. While resting in bed that afternoon I began reading the book, *Man's Search for Meaning*, that George had given me. A large portion of the book was about author Viktor Frankl's experience being imprisoned in Auschwitz. Frankl explained how difficult it is to maintain the will to live when people are stripped of everything tying them to their past life. With the loss of their clothes and even their hair, all that remained was a "naked existence." The people who were able to maintain their humanity in these conditions were usually the ones who survived the longest. With no intention whatsoever of comparing my personal struggles to the Holocaust, the idea of losing that which defines you reminded me of muscular dystrophy. There was little doubt that one day my ability to walk would be diminished, and I would need people to help me with basic tasks. How does one maintain a positive mindset with that lingering in their future? I did not have an answer. This mental environment is comparable to wearing a ticking time bomb without seeing the clock, constantly wondering how much time is left. The difficulties in dealing with a burden like this stem from an expectation that life should play out a certain way. We can expect nothing but the life we have been given.

The next morning as I left Agés, the trail elevation began to rise again. My calves and shins began to cramp as I struggled up the hill. The stiffness in my shins was known as a shin splint, a painful occurrence that causes difficulty walking and raising the feet. My theory as to why I often suffer from shin splints is because my Achilles tendons are tight due to muscular dystrophy, causing me to rely more on my shins. Walking up the steep hill the day before must have tired out my shins.

I sat down beside a lichen-covered stone trail marker to rest. In my head, I told myself this was the last big hill for a while. If I could make it over this hill, I could at least make it through the flat Meseta before the mountains at the end of the Camino. After a few minutes, my shin pain subsided, and I continued walking. My usual physical difficulties were mentally a little easier to manage today, since my intestinal issues finally ended that morning. Having one less thing to worry about was refreshing.

As I slowly climbed higher, the ground became bare grey rock. The crumbling and jagged nature of the stones required me to step from rock to rock and use my hiking pole as an anchor. Several places nearly caused me to crawl, but there were a few washed out areas of dirt along the side of the trail where I could walk around.

While I was walking through one of these sections, an older stout woman wearing a bandana over her head and walking with her husband who sported a full white beard stopped and looked at me. The woman was wearing a small pack with little more than a water bottle and some basic supplies, but the husband had an unusually large pack. He was most likely carrying both of their possessions. With an Eastern European accent, the woman asked me if I was alright. After explaining I had muscular dystrophy, the wife told me they were from Serbia, and that she had cancer and was hiking the Camino before she died. My initial thought was to say how sorry I was to hear that, but I hesitated. She was not on the Camino to feel sorry for herself; she was here to live. Thinking back to my thoughts while reading Frankl's book, I realized the difficulty with facing an impending doom stems from focusing on what we are losing and not what we have. We only have the time we have now. People grow through challenges and even until our dying breath we can find meaning in life.

"I'm happy to hear that you are here," I said with a smile.

"Thank you. I'm glad you are able to walk too."

I walked with them for a few moments, but their pace was much quicker than mine, and they moved ahead. Before they left, they both said "ultreia," instead of the usual "Buen Camino." This was a saying I read about, but had never heard used. This Spanish word has no direct translation to English, but means to travel beyond. To say ultreia is not to wish someone a safe journey to Santiago, but instead a safe journey in a spiritual transformation. The Finnish phrase "jaksaa, jaksaa" that Ella spoke of towards the beginning of the Camino always reminded me of ultreia, as it implies that strength has a much deeper meaning than the physical capacities of our bodies.

After just under a mile of the torturous ground, I came to a barren landscape as the clouds were beginning to break and a golden sunrise lit up the sky. A wooden cross about twenty feet tall anchored in a large pile of rocks marked the top of the hill. I saw the Serbian couple tossing stones on the top of the pile. With their rocks added to the mound, they held hands and gazed at the cross as I stood next to them. The husband turned to me and said, "Did you bring a rock to leave your burden behind?"

I knew right away that he mistakenly thought this was a location known as Cruz de Ferro. That place is much farther on the Camino where pilgrims place a stone in a large pile of rocks around an iron cross affixed atop a large wooden pole. The rock is meant to represent leaving behind a burden brought from one's life before the Camino. After I explained to the couple the mistake they had made, they looked heart-broken knowing they placed their rocks on the wrong pile. Trying to reassure them I said, "I guess it does not matter where you leave behind your burdens on the Camino. Perhaps you were meant to leave them here."

The woman gave me a hug and said, "You give me strength."

They moved on ahead, and I never saw them again. Later that evening after I arrived in the big city of Burgos I sat at an outdoor cafe and ate a personal pizza and tall beer in celebration of making it to the Meseta. While I ate, I texted Florence and Alma to let them know I was in the city, and they both said they would come to meet me right away. Florence was staying in a hotel down the street, and she arrived within minutes.

"Bryan!" I heard Florence's voice call out, and I looked up to see her walking over at a slow pace. She had a bright smile, but her eyes did not have the usual optimistic glow I remembered. I stood up and gave her a hug before she sat down and ordered a beer from the waiter who was cleaning the adjacent table. Florence crossed her arms, looked down at the tabletop and paused for a moment before she began explaining the progression of her knee injury that began during the last few days we walked together.

"You were right that day I walked all the way to Los Arcos. I should have stayed with you in Villamayor. That long day did me in."

I responded, "You're not the only one. Burgos seems to be the place where a lot of injuries bring people down."

Florence continued to say, "I could push on and see how much farther I could go, but the Camino isn't worth an injury I'll regret for the rest of my life. I'll come back in a few years and pick up where I left off here in Burgos."

Alma arrived shortly after Florence, and we both gave her a big hug. Her eyes were tearing when she sat down. Her expression told many feelings from being happy to see me to being upset to end her Camino. This was her sixth time walking on the Camino, and the first time she intended to walk the entire distance. She had such high hopes when I first met her that I was surprised her journey came to an end like Florence's. After talking about everything that transpired since I last saw her, she said, "I felt so bad leaving you in Uterga, but it makes me happy to know you have made it this far. I have no doubt you will make it to Santiago."

Alma explained how Beth decided to rent a bike to ride through the Meseta, and Alma was taking a bus to León the next day to meet her there. There was a heavy disappointment in Alma's eyes when she talked about being forced to stop and Beth going ahead of her, but she was happy for Beth. The three of us talked for over an hour, but Florence was not feeling well, so she went back to her hotel to sleep. She was taking a flight to England the next day where she planned to do some sightseeing for the remainder of her time in Europe. We would keep in touch after we parted ways, but she became another person who had woven in and out of my journey.

After Florence left, Alma and I walked down the street

to see the Burgos Cathedral with its towering spires that resembled a castle. This cathedral, which began construction in 1221, was not finished until the 18th century and was the second largest in Spain. Made of limestone quarried from the surrounding land, it was built in the classic Gothic style of the Renaissance. The architecture was unlike anything else I encountered on the Camino and was more reminiscent of Rome or the Vatican. We walked around the exterior, taking pictures and admiring the marvelous structure. There were no tours this late in the day, but we walked inside and were able to see several large stone pillars connecting to a tall ceiling with intricate glass chandeliers. Never in my life had I seen architecture of this magnitude.

After a brief stroll through the Cathedral's gift shop where Alma purchased postcards to send home to Norway, the time had come for us to part ways for the last time on the Camino. Alma promised to give Beth my regards when she met her in León tomorrow. As we walked back to my albergue, Alma wiped a few tears from her eyes. Being with her felt like seeing an aunt or distant relative. Even if I failed to reach Santiago, the people I met had already left a lasting mark on my life.

Burgos felt like a turning point in my Camino. I persevered through physical obstacles, faced the unknown, battled sickness and bed bugs, and wondered how much more my body was capable of withstanding. Even though there were still questions in my mind, there was nothing I needed to truly fear at this point. The journey would take me where it needed to take me. Though the Meseta would be less physically demanding, the real struggle was approaching. The journey would become more inward, beyond fear, beyond doubt, and into the true meaning of strength.

7

THE MESETA

When I left Burgos on the morning of September 4, I entered the Meseta, which stretched for about 140 miles. I planned to spend twelve days crossing this desolate, flat landscape. This section of the Camino is often described as the most emotionally difficult section. Unbroken stretches of trail sometimes create a feeling of no progress being made. For me, the Meseta was to become my favorite part of the Camino. The level ground gave my muscles a much needed rest before the mountains toward the end of the trail.

As I approached an outdoor cafe in the village of Tardajos I heard someone call my name. I looked up and saw a German man in his mid-fifties with thick spectacles and a wide grin. His name was Roland, and I had met him briefly at my albergue in the town of Agés several days before. I remembered him telling stories of his time hitchhiking and following the band The Eagles throughout the United States in the 1970s. He was sitting with his wife Helen, who brushed the brown hair out of her eyes and looked up at me with a weak smile. Helen looked to be about twenty years younger than Roland.

"Here, come and eat with us," Roland said, and pointed to an empty chair. His excited tone indicated this was not a suggestion but a demand. I was not very hungry but figured this would be a good place for an early lunch. After putting my pack and hiking pole down on the chair, I entered the small café and ordered a bocadillo jamón. The woman at the counter did not make eye contact, quickly called my order out to the back kitchen, and moved on to the customers behind me. This was clearly the first open café since Burgos and nearly every pilgrim stopped here.

Back outside at the table, Roland asked, "Where are you headed today?"

"Hornillos. Not much farther from here."

"Yes, yes, yes, us as well. Which albergue? We are staying at an albergue called Meeting Point," Roland said quickly.

"Didn't have any plans. I'll stay there then."

"Yes, yes, yes. I hear they cook delicious paella for dinner. And now you are staying there too, so it will be an excellent time."

My sandwich was much smaller than expected, but was on a crispy toasted roll with thick slices of meat that were easy to chew. Roland was still drinking coffee and eating eggs when I was ready to continue. Helen finished her meal and sat with her hands folded.

"There's never a sense of haste with you is there," Helen said to Roland. Roland laughed and said, "I'm just taking it all in. Why don't you walk with Bryan? I'll be done soon."

"Fine," Helen said, and she pushed in her chair and put on her pack.

"We'll see you up ahead then," I said.

"Yes. Don't wait up for me though. We're all going to Hornillos."

After only a few minutes of walking with Helen, she began to complain about her feet hurting, how hot it was, and about how much she wanted to be finished with the Camino. She and Roland were only walking to León and were planning to return the next year to finish the walk to Santiago.

"I am sorry, but my feet hurt more when I walk slowly. I will go ahead," Helen said abruptly. She increased her pace and moved on.

The Meseta

I wondered how Roland maintained such a happy-go-lucky attitude with Helen constantly complaining. My first reaction was to tell her that this was the reason people walk the Camino. If you come with the expectation that everything will be easy, you are doomed to have a miserable time. Even though I was initially overwhelmed, much like Helen, my added challenges taught me to accept the difficulties. Trying to maintain a certain degree of comfort is the best way to lose all comfort. Maybe my feet hurt, my legs were tired, and my body was itching from bug bites, but I was alive and very much aware of it. Establishing this mindset is what saved me from the misery that Helen and so many others experienced.

After Helen moved ahead, I continued through Tardajos and into the adjacent Rabé de las Calzadas. There had been a change in the architecture since Burgos. The homes were built in an adobe style that reminded me of Mexico or the American Southwest. Everything in Tardajos and Rabé de las Calzadas had a dusty and faded look, from the cement streets to the red clay shingles.

As I passed the last buildings of the settlement, and the final outskirts of Burgos gave way to nature and farmland, I paused for a moment. There were no more mountains on the horizon. The gravel trail stretched into the distance behind several low rolling hills. The land was dry and the fields were plowed, revealing the end of summer and the coming of fall. In the sky were white billowy cumulus clouds, looking like cotton candy, in front of a backdrop of vibrant blue. The heat had increased now that noon was approaching, and the sun lit up the landscape, occasionally casting shadows that rolled across the land. This was the Meseta, and there was something sacred and holy about the view. The rocky road was etched deep into the ground; traversed for over a millennium as people made the same pilgrimage as me. Alongside the trail were hilly embankments with large rocks, dry shrubs, and weeds. Something about the Meseta's flat, semi-arid landscape was familiar. Maybe this was what I imagined when I pictured myself walking on the Camino.

My feet began to burn as the afternoon went on, and after taking a short rest in the shade of a small tree, Roland caught up to me and immediately uplifted my spirits. He always had a wide smile and continuous energy that lit up the world around him like the sun. His bright blue eyes pierced through his glasses, giving him the persona of a witty college professor. He explained that he was a retired school teacher, which was a fitting career for him.

Just as Hornillos came into view, the trail led down a slight incline where the rocks were rounded and slippery. The bottom of my shoe caught one of the rocks. I went down hard, but Roland did not panic and simply put his hand out and pulled me up to my feet in one simple motion. Usually, I expected a panic from whomever I was with, like I experienced during my first fall with Beth and Alma, but Roland had such a cool attitude that nothing fazed him. Though I was not asked, I felt inclined to explain that I had muscular dystrophy.

"Ah okay. Not to worry, we are on the Camino together. I will help you."

When we arrived at our albergue in Hornillos, Helen was sitting on a bench by the front door. Her expression looked neutral, and she did not appear to be excited to see us.

Roland and Helen spoke to each other in German for a minute, then Roland turned to me with a smile and said, "Well, shall we enter?"

The three of us walked inside and into the entry room that was dark and cool. A young woman with long brown hair smiled and directed us to immediately take off our sneakers and put them on an empty shelf, revealing we were the first pilgrims to arrive. Back at the check-in desk, I asked the woman if I could be assigned to a bottom bunk.

"Yes," the woman laughed.

As she looked at my credential and pointed at my date of

birth, she asked, "You were born in 1993, and you are asking for a bottom bunk?"

"I'm sorry, but I have muscular dystrophy, and I can't climb onto the top bunks," I said bluntly.

"Oh, I am sorry. I did not know," she said in an embarrassed tone.

As much as I was annoyed by her comment, these types of interactions were normal. I always received weird looks when I took elevators up one floor and nothing appeared to be wrong with me. People are always so quick to judge someone without knowing any information about them. After the woman checked us in, she walked us upstairs to the beds.

"Are you okay walking up the steps?" the woman asked, as she put her hand on my shoulder. I could tell she was trying to make up for the awkward exchange we just had.

"Yeah, I'm alright," I said.

"Do you want me to carry your pack up the steps?" Roland asked.

"You don't have to if . . ." I hardly had the words out of my mouth, and Roland took my pack and carried it up the steps while still wearing his own.

Later that afternoon as the albergue began to fill up, I was hanging my laundry outside to dry and ran into a pilgrim named Rebecca from South Africa. I met her briefly in Grañón when I was sick. She had a better memory of me than I did of her, and she asked, "How are you feeling?"

"Oh, I'm alright," I said.

"Weren't you sick?"

"Oh yes. I forgot you were there that night. I'm finally better now!"

"That's good! I had a little upset stomach a couple days ago. I thought of you, and hoped I wasn't going to be brought down like that."

Rebecca and I sat on some white plastic chairs in the shade of the building. We chatted about our lives while we waited for our clothes to dry. Rebecca was twenty-eight years old and recently quit her flight attendant job in Dubai. The long hours and unpredictable schedule became too stressful for her. She returned home to South Africa before deciding to walk the Camino.

"I thought I would do this now before I'm too old, when this would be considered a mid-life crisis and not just still figuring myself out. Loads of people do this, so I figured it was worth a try," Rebecca said.

"How did you first hear about the Camino?" I asked.

"To be honest I read about it in a magazine on a flight from Dubai to Madrid about a year ago. I thought it sounded cool. And here I am with the time to do it, so I'm doing it. How about you?"

"I really don't have a definitive moment I heard about it. I was always aware of many trails like the Camino around the world and just kind of always had it in the back of my mind. This year I decided I wanted to do a long hike, so I decided on the Camino."

"Interesting. I always like hearing about why people wind up here. Or maybe it helps me feel less bad about my own decision."

Rebecca went on to explain how over the past few days, she had been suffering from a self-diagnosed stress fracture in her right shin that had become very painful. The pain she described sounded like the shin splints that I had experienced several times. According to Rebecca, shin splints could lead to a stress fracture if overexertion is continued. The next day she planned to take advantage of a backpack transfer service to send her pack ahead to the next albergue she was staying at. After she told me about her struggle with a stress fracture, I went on to explain my experience walking the Camino with muscular dystrophy. She did not have much to say in response, which was refreshing after telling my background to countless pilgrims.

The Meseta

A little while later Roland came outside and sat down in a nearby chair in a huff. This behavior surprised me, since I had yet to see him without a smile. He noticed my expression as I read his actions and said, "Well, as you can see I'm not happy now."

"What happened?"

"Oh, you know, it's Helen. We just had a little disagreement."

I was not surprised and responded, "Well, she looked like she had a difficult day today."

"That's the thing. We all went through the same things today. It's just her mindset. Helen should be walking with you. She needs inspiration to learn to deal with pain."

I felt a little weird being described as an object of inspiration. Because of my strong drive to keep walking, people I met on the Camino tended to think I had everything figured out. I made sure not to take Roland's comment personally, since I could tell he was frustrated.

"It takes time to develop the right mindset. I'm still working through a lot of issues," I said in response.

"We came on the Camino to become closer, but now we hardly walk together and only talk briefly at the end of the day once we reach our albergue," Roland said, with a heavy sigh.

Rebecca then said, "The Camino heals, so maybe this is part of the healing process. Sometimes the words we say need to be said."

"I hope so," Roland said.

"Maybe you cannot see it now, but when you go home, you will see how much you grew together," Rebecca said.

I sat with my new acquaintances at the albergue dinner and had pleasant conversation, but Helen appeared miserable and kept to herself. I wondered if she would be able to find some joy in the Camino experience. For now, I was happy to finally be in the Meseta and in a new wave of pilgrims. I was looking forward to the next several days.

My Own Pace

The next morning I walked off and on with Roland. I did not see Helen and wondered where she was. Roland did not mention anything about her, so I did not ask. We entered the town of Hontanas around noon and spotted a cafe for lunch. The establishment looked recently built with a beaded doorway under a fabric awning with several tables and chairs in the front. Rebecca, who was sitting at one of the tables, immediately saw us and ushered us over to join her. I ordered a bocadillo jamón and Roland ordered two large egg bocadillos and a tall beer. After sitting down, I asked Rebecca, "How are your shins feeling after walking this morning?"

"Good. Sending my pack ahead really seemed to help."

"That's good. Where did you send your pack to?"

"I'm not sure. It was a municipal albergue in Castrojeriz. I'll figure it out when I get there."

"I'm stopping in Castrojeriz too, but I'm going to stop in the first albergue I find."

Roland chimed in with a mouthful of bocadillo and said, "Me as well. Don't know where I'm stopping this time either. Helen and I want to find a hotel tonight."

"How are you guys doing today?" Rebecca asked.

"Better. We talked last night, and I think we're doing well. We're still walking at our own paces today, but we're good," Roland said.

Roland went back to eating and reading his guidebook, and his eyes lit up.

"Oh, did you know in this very town, there apparently lives a man named Victorino, who entertains pilgrims by pouring wine on his forehead, inhaling through his nose, and pouring it back out through his mouth?"

"That sounds disgusting," Rebecca said with a soft chuckle.

"This is incredible! I must find Victorino," Roland said.

The café host was cleaning the table next to us and overheard, adding, "Victorino is retired. He no do that anymore."

"Nonsense. I am Victorino!" Roland belted out in an operatic voice.

"I'll pay to see you try!" a young woman with an Australian accent called out from a nearby table.

"Ha! There is no doubt in my mind I was born to do this."

"I have a bottle of wine," the Australian woman said, as she tucked her long blond hair behind her ear, and reached down into her pack to pull out an unopened bottle of red wine. Roland walked over to the woman and held the bottle up in the air.

"Behold, the great Victorino!" Roland shouted out, just as Helen arrived at the café with a bright smile. I realized this was the first time I saw her with a genuine smile.

"Do I even want to know what I walked into?" she asked.

"Of course, of course, just in time to be my assistant! Hold this cup," Roland responded, as he grabbed an empty cup off of the Australian's table and handed it to Helen. The Australian woman opened the bottle, and Roland took off his glasses and rested them on the table. The half dozen pilgrims at the café now had their attention fixated on Roland. His personality always captivated those around him. I knew I could meet a million more people in my life and never meet another man like Roland. The café host took little interest in the excitement, as he probably saw countless drunken pilgrims attempt this feat.

Helen held the cup under Roland's mouth as he slowly lifted the wine bottle into the air. He paused for a moment with the bottle tilted inches away from a stream of wine pouring out.

"And now ladies and gentlemen, we shall go where no German has gone before."

The wine appeared to flow in slow motion as the stream hit his forehead and ran down his face. Splashing all over his head and running down his neck, the red wine drenched his grey shirt. Both laughing and coughing from wine that dripped into his mouth, he grabbed the cup from Helen's hand and poured wine directly into the cup.

"I have made wine into the cup," Roland belted out as he put the wine bottle down on the table and thrust the cup up into the air.

All of the pilgrims at the café clapped and cheered at the failed attempt. The Australian woman went inside the café and brought out wine glasses for all the pilgrims present and poured everyone a small glass.

"To Victorino!" I exclaimed, and we all clinked glasses.

Helen laughed at everything Roland said as they conversed in German. Rebecca had already finished her food and left a few minutes later. I was ready to leave shortly after and Roland promised to see me again in Castrojeriz that evening or on the trail tomorrow. Sadly, I would not see him again. Another friend had come and gone on the Camino.

On my way out of Hontanas to complete the last six miles of my day, I spotted a middle-aged man wearing an American flag bandana and taking a picture of the open landscape ahead of us. He was broad-shouldered and husky, with a neatly trimmed salt and pepper colored beard, wearing a black baseball hat and a button-up blue shirt.

I said hello when I passed him. His eyes lit up and he said in an excited tone, "Hey, where are you from?"

"New Jersey. How about you?"

"Oh, no way! I am originally from Harrisburg, Pennsylvania. Where about in New Jersey?"

"Trenton. So not too far away."

"Ah, nice. I've been there several times. I live in Arizona now, but I'm still on the East Coast fairly often. Looks like you have a nice walking pace going. Did you start in St-Jean?"

"Yeah, and you?" I asked.

"Yup, I am taking my time though. I'm the slowest pilgrim on the Camino."

The Meseta

"Nah, I think I'm the slowest person on the Camino," I laughed.

"What? A young guy like you? No one is slower than an old fat man like me," he said.

"I have muscular dystrophy, so I'm forced to go slow."

"No way! That's great, man! I mean . . . that's great that you are out here on the Camino."

"Thanks. I'm just walking while I still can."

"Incredible! What's your name, man?"

"Bryan, and you?"

"My name is Isaac. I stop to take a million pictures of everything, so I'm not going to hold you up," he said abruptly, and stopped to take another picture.

"It was nice to meet you Isaac," I said, and I continued on.

As I walked away he called out, "Looks like I'm still the slowest person on the Camino."

"I guess it's going to be a competition," I laughed.

The Camino continued on a narrow rocky trail alongside an old stone wall with weeds and dry grass growing out of the holes and cracks. On the other side of the trail was a barren hill with large scattered stones that were most likely remnants of ancient ruins. After about two miles on this trail, the Camino led back onto the paved road through the shade of several small trees that cast cooling shadows on the road. The surrounding landscape was flat, with plowed fields, and a handful of rocky hills on the horizon.

One of the fields by the side of the road had soft green grass blanketed in the shade of a tree. Seeing this as an ideal place for a rest, I lay down in the grass and closed my eyes for a few minutes. The sound of the light breeze rustling through the trees and a few chirping birds made me want to fall asleep. A voice suddenly broke through the stillness and said, "Looks like a cool spot for a nap."

I opened my eyes to see Isaac walking toward me.

"I couldn't resist," I said, as I stood up to greet him.

"I didn't mean to disturb you," Isaac said quickly.

"No, it's fine. I was ready to get moving anyway."

"Hey, did you meet a woman on the Camino named Eleanor from Texas?" Isaac asked.

"Yes, I did!" I said.

"I thought so. I saw her the other day. She mentioned you by name, Bryan from New Jersey who is walking out here with muscular dystrophy. She was moved by you," Isaac said.

"Oh, wow that's great. She was such a sweet woman," I said.

I was surprised Eleanor talked about me to other pilgrims. Those few hours I walked with her over a week earlier must have had an incredible impact. I remembered she took down my information to find me on Facebook, but I never heard anything from her. Hopefully I would run into her again soon. When I think back to everyone I met on the Camino, I realized that only a small selection of people were the ones I would actually remember. In this sense, walking with someone for a couple hours was enough time to make an impression. The people I remembered probably remembered me with similar regard.

Isaac said that he worked remotely from his cell phone and was able to travel the world while he worked. He was glad to see a young person like me on the Camino, and he planned to return with his daughter when she graduated from high school the next year. I walked with Isaac until we came to the ruins of a cathedral complex along the side of the road. Known as Convento de San Annton, this structure was built in the 11th century and was a well-known stop along the Camino during the Middle Ages. As we approached the ruins, we saw a massive stone archway that crossed over the road between two halves of the ruins. Inside, the ceiling and sections of the front and rear wall were missing, and the floor was bare ground with clumps of grass around the base of the walls. I envisioned a once beautiful cathedral with chandeliers, a gold altar, and rows of pews. The empty window frames must have once held intricate stained glass. I could almost hear a choir of ghosts echoing off the stone walls. Now the only sounds were chirping birds and the wind as it continued to erode the crumbling structure. Today, a small albergue with no running water or electricity is maintained in a refurbished section of the ruins.

"Do you know what these massive cathedrals represent?" Isaac asked.

"No, what?" I questioned.

"Faith!" Isaac exclaimed in an excited tone, continuing to say, "Thousands of years ago a man had a vision to build a cathedral right here. He employed his entire family and created a community to erect this building, knowing he would never see it completed, knowing his children would probably never see it completed, with faith that in several generations there would be a cathedral here."

"That's a beautiful way to look at it. I'm sure he never envisioned these ruins though."

"Probably not, but a man's vision once stood here. It doesn't matter if you believe in God or not, this is an example of faith anyone can believe in."

After snapping a few pictures, Isaac decided to stop for a cold drink. The albergue looked inviting with a beaded doorway and Buddhist prayer flags draped outside, but I was less than three miles from my destination and wanted to get going. I said goodbye to Isaac and continued onward.

That evening when I was napping in my bed at my albergue, I heard another pilgrim enter the room. I opened my eyes to see a familiar face. It was Eleanor from Texas. I silently laughed to myself at the coincidence of seeing her so soon after Isaac had mentioned her.

"Eleanor!" I exclaimed after she put her pack down next to a bed and looked around the room.

My Own Pace

"Bryan!" she said, as she hurried over and gave me a hug. "I'm so glad I ran into you again. I tried to find you on Facebook but didn't have any luck. How are you? How have you been?"

As she got settled, we talked about everything that had happened since we parted ways. I told her I ran into Isaac and how he mentioned her.

"Oh, I'm so happy you were able to meet him. He is such a cool guy," she beamed.

Once Eleanor was settled in, she offered to buy me a beer at the albergue café. I graciously accepted. We sat outside in the courtyard, drank our beer, and chatted. She was able to find me on Facebook so we could keep in touch.

"You must have strong faith in God to be out here on your own," she said, with a smile.

I paused for a moment to think about my response. The idea of God was once again presented to me on the Camino as something I should have had without question. I was still unsure how to navigate that conversation. My faith in reaching Santiago remained strong, and I was greatly moved by the kindness of strangers, but this was not necessarily finding God in the Christian sense of the word. There was something I spoke to in moments of contemplation, some may call that God, but I do not know if anyone was listening, or if maybe the God I envisioned was already within me. I thought about how Naomi explained God by stating, "There are more ways to believe in God than there are people on Earth . . . but you do not have to believe in God to believe in God." A divine intervention was not necessary to discover God. I just needed to find my own way. Faith could take on other forms, such as building a cathedral like Isaac explained.

Replying to Eleanor's statement, I said, "I'm not really sure if I believe in God."

"Oh, I'm sorry, I did not mean any offense by that."

"No, no it's okay. I mean, I needed some sort of faith to

make it these past two hundred miles. So I'm still a very spiritual person, being on the Camino and everything."

"Well, I was raised a Southern Baptist, but the Catholic Church is a beautiful thing. Being out here on the Camino, I feel the love of God all around."

"Yes, there is something truly spiritual about this place."

Though we parted ways on the Camino after that evening, I hoped our paths would cross again. The thought that you might run into someone again is a moving force. There is always a little bit of faith that maybe this person has a bigger role to play before the journey ends. Even though I would never see Eleanor again, there were still many other people who would make a reappearance.

I slept well during my night in Castrojeriz but was awake by 5:00 the next morning and decided to get an early start. At the edge of town, after crossing a bridge over a small river, the trail immediately rose in elevation as I approached a hill called Alto de Mostelares. There was a warning sign at the base of the hill indicating a twelve percent grade. This was the first time I ever came across a sign showing the steepness of the trail. Though it was less than a mile to the top, it was steeper than the Pyrenees. Even with the light of my headlamp, I could not see more than a few dozen feet ahead. The trail was so steep that I could barely lift each leg before my shoe made contact with the ground. My shins became stiff and painful with each step, making it nearly impossible to raise my foot. I thought of Rebecca with her stress fracture and hoped I was not experiencing the same problem.

I used the technique of walking backwards to give some of my muscles a break and pushed myself up with my hiking pole as I ascended the hill. I peered back every few steps to make sure I was still on the trail and I continued uphill with the view of the lights of Castrojeriz visible in the distance. There was a slight glow on the horizon as sunrise neared, and I saw the headlamps of other pilgrims making their way up the trail. As people approached, I turned back around so I would not shine my light in their eyes. Everyone was pretty quiet, as this hill was a struggle for them as well. Every few minutes I would stop to catch my breath and hope the top was near.

Finally, after an hour of walking, I felt the relief of flat ground as I crested the top. Strong wind whipped at my jacket, and I made sure my hat was secured tightly. There was a small stone shelter at the top with several benches under a shingled roof. At high noon, the structure would have been a welcome relief from the heat, but at the moment I wanted to be warm as my fingers became numb from the wind. The sun broke through the horizon just as I looked back on the trail I climbed. Across the checkerboard of farm fields, I could see castle ruins on a hill next to Castrojeriz. To the south, across a distant ridgeline, was a row of about fifty wind turbines reflecting sun rays through a slight haze of clouds.

I continued across the flat top of the hill, which had a large expanse of plowed farm fields. There was no definitive peak on the ridge, looking rather like someone sliced off the top of the hill. A few hundred feet from the shelter, the trail suddenly dropped off with an even steeper eighteen percent grade going down. The paved trail ran to the edge of the horizon across seemingly endless farmland. The next town, Itero de la Vega, was visible five miles away, and beyond that I could barely see my destination Boadilla, still over nine miles away.

The walk downhill was easier with the help of gravity but more terrifying. One fall here would undoubtedly result in a long tumble and several broken bones. I leaned backwards as I inched down on my toes, placing my hiking pole continuously in front of me. Midway to the bottom I heard someone call out my name and was surprised to see Rebecca approaching from behind me.

"I was thinking about you the whole way up this hill. I guess you made it alright?" she asked.

"Yeah, it was steep, but I made it. I was thinking about

you too. My shins were hurting, and I was hoping it was not a stress fracture, but I'm alright now. How's your fracture feeling?"

"Much better now. Sending my backpack ahead still seems to be helping."

Rebecca stopped for a rest after coming down the hill, but I continued on my own for a while. Later in the afternoon after my lunch break, I heard Rebecca's voice from behind me.

"Oh, I am so happy to see you. I was walking with the most horrible woman who was getting on my nerves and made me itch all over," she asserted.

Rebecca described a blond-haired American woman in her mid-thirties who I remembered seeing at my albergue the night before. The distinctive whiny voice that Rebecca imitated was exactly how I remembered her. She seemed rude when I overheard her talking to a few other pilgrims from afar, and what Rebecca went on to describe confirmed my opinion.

"She told me I should be ashamed for being a white South African because of the apartheid. The nerve of this woman!" Rebecca exclaimed.

I laughed at the irony and said, "You should have asked her if she felt ashamed for being a white American."

"I know. I was thinking that. And then she went on to say that since I was twenty-eight and single, I was probably never going to get married, so I should just give up on men," Rebecca continued.

"It's strange to find someone on the Camino who is so negative. Usually people are more upbeat than that," I said.

Rebecca agreed and said, "I told her how it sounded like she had a lot of built-up anger inside of her, and she said, 'I know, the reason I'm angry is because of men.'"

"I don't understand how people just release their anger on other people, like she did on you. It's annoying," I said.

"Maybe she just needs to talk to someone like you. Go rub off some of your positive vibes on her," she laughed.

111

"It's funny that I got the same vibe from her last night without even talking to her."

"Well, people give off the emotions they feel on the inside. You can't judge a book by its cover, but reading the back cover is usually a good place to start."

I laughed and said, "Yeah, you're not wrong. You get the synopsis of someone within a few minutes of conversation."

"Well, if I was a book, do you think I would be worth a read from the cover?" Rebecca said, as she flicked her blond hair to the side and framed her face with the back of her hand on her chin.

"That's a tough one. I'm not particularly sure," I said, with a condescending smile.

Rebecca laughed and kicked up some dust on my feet and said, "I hate you."

As we neared Boadilla, Rebecca explained how she was not stopping there and was continuing on to the next town. She needed to quicken her pace if she was to reach Santiago within her timeframe. Rebecca recommended an albergue in Boadilla called En el Camino that was owned by a local artist.

"I was really looking forward to staying there, but I can't keep doing twenty kilometers a day if I want to finish. My shin is feeling better now, so I'm going to move on," Rebecca said.

When we reached the dusty, quiet Boadilla around 1:00, we found the albergue in the town square across from a faded dome-shaped stone church. Inside the adobe albergue was a large courtyard with bright green grass and a small shallow in-ground swimming pool surrounded by dozens of metal sculptures mostly depicting pilgrims with walking sticks. The buildings around the courtyard were light yellow with low roofs, looking like cottages in the countryside.

"Oh, this place is beautiful. Maybe I should stay here," Rebecca said as she looked around.

"Well, I'm staying here."

The Meseta

Rebecca frowned with an expression of uncertainty, "There's always going to be that one place you wish you stayed. This is that place for me."

"Well, this is where we part ways then. It's been nice walking with you over the past few days," I said.

"Yeah, you've really helped me on this journey. I realize there's nothing we can't do if we really want it. If I don't see you again, good luck, Godspeed and Buen Camino."

"Thanks, same to you. Buen Camino," I responded as we hugged.

There is always a crushing feeling inside when you meet someone really interesting and then they fade into the horizon. This is the nature of the Camino. Every time you meet someone, you never know if they will be there for five minutes or all the way to Santiago.

I followed a slate path through the courtyard to the café, where several pilgrims were gathered at outdoor seating. I walked into the dimly lit building where another pilgrim was sitting at a table being checked in by a man in his mid-thirties with well-groomed black hair, a short shadowy beard, and a deep, booming Spanish accent.

After I was checked in and paid for a bed, I predictably ordered a bocadillo jamón. Before my food was ready, the host directed me and the other pilgrim to the dorm area to pick a bed. We first entered a lounge area with dark red walls and a wood-beamed ceiling. The room was filled with several tables surrounded by leather chairs. In one corner was an old wood-burning stove and all four walls had paintings of Meseta landscapes. After we passed through the entry room, we were shown a long room with about twenty sets of bunks. The beds were packed tightly together, and I knew the snoring would be incredible tonight.

I put my belongings down, claimed a bottom bunk, and hurried back to the café to eat my bocadillo. When I re-entered the café, I saw Isaac sitting at a table eating an apple.

"Isaac!" I said, as I sat down at a table with him.

"Bryan! How are you man? You staying here tonight?"

"Yeah. You?"

"Yes and no. I got a private room at the hotel portion of the albergue next door."

As we spoke, a flood of pilgrims began to arrive. The host frantically ran back and forth checking people in and showing them to the room. One girl around my age who looked to be about three hundred pounds, with brown hair pulled back under a blue bandana, dropped her pack and sprawled out onto the ground. The look of utter exhaustion on her face was simply indescribable as she huffed for breath and sweat dripped from her forehead.

"I give someone like that so much credit for coming out here," Isaac said.

"Yeah, I can't even imagine how difficult it is for her being so overweight."

"Even with your condition, you think it's harder for her?"

I did not know how to respond and simply said, "I certainly never looked that beat up at the end of the day."

Isaac chuckled in response and said, "It's inspiring in a strange way, to see someone push through obstacles to show their true strength."

"Yeah, I guess so. Everyone has difficulties in their lives, but difficulties just manifest themselves in different ways. I've met people with less physical hardship who are more unhappy than me, as well as people with more handicaps who are happier than me."

"That's real interesting, man. I never really thought about it that way. It's like I always say, everyone has potential, but it's only a matter of finding the right place to channel that potential."

I talked with Isaac for a few minutes until he said, "Well, I'd love to stay and talk, but I need to take a shower and wash some clothes before the machines get filled up." We wished each other well. This would be the last time I saw Isaac on the Camino.

The next three days after I left Boadilla were relatively uneventful as I found myself in a new wave of passing pilgrims. Because of my slow pace on the Camino, I never walked with the same people for more than a few days before they passed me. I would usually talk to other pilgrims in the albergues in the evenings, but as I made my way farther on the Camino, I discovered pilgrims generally had less of a desire to talk to each other. Everyone's life stories eventually begin to blend together, and a lot of pilgrims start to seem the same. The Meseta continued to be refreshing for me since the flat landscape presented few physical obstacles. I tried to keep my mind off the upcoming mountains beyond the Meseta and just focused on my own pace, but I would not have to wait long before the Camino threw another unexpected challenge at me.

8

THE HALFWAY MARK

On my twenty-third day on the trail, I passed a cement marker that read: "Geographical Center of the Camino de Santiago." Though I had already crossed the halfway point based on mileage that morning, in a geographical sense I was now halfway between St-Jean and Santiago. From the marker, the Camino continued into the town Sahagún. This town was the first place on the Camino that felt unsafe. The many graffiti-ridden buildings and streets walled with beggars made me want to pass through as quickly as I could. After arriving in the mid-afternoon, I stayed in my albergue the rest of the day.

I slipped out of the albergue around 5:30 the next morning. Even though it was only an eight mile day, my body was stuck on an early rising schedule. My goal was to have breakfast three miles away in Calzade de Coto by 7:00 and be at my destination in Calzadilla de los Hermanillos by 10:00. Feeling confident in my plans, I did not bother to look over the guidebook before I set out. As I made my way down the sidewalk, in the shadow of a building across the street I saw a man dressed in black with his face hidden in a hood. He looked up as I neared and walked across the street toward me and mumbled something in Spanish. His long sleeves were rolled up revealing both arms covered with tattoos. I guessed he was in his early thirties.

The Halfway Mark

"No hablo Español," I said, trying to avoid any more talk.

He then spoke in English, "You have a cigarette, my friend?"

"Nah sorry," I said, as I kept walking. He stepped in front of me and put his hand on my shoulder.

"You pilgrim?"

"Yeah," I said, as I pushed his hand off my shoulder and kept walking. He stood still as I moved away from him at a quicker pace.

"Americano?" he asked, as I tried to increase my distance from him.

I made my way across a stone bridge and looked over my shoulder to see him approaching at a fast pace. He yelled something in Spanish, and I sensed ill intent in his voice. Knowing I could not outrun him, I looked around at my surroundings. To my left was a farm with a grove of trees in perfect rows. This was a place I could hide. I pushed through a thick patch of tall grass and hurried into the trees.

After about fifty feet, I took my pack off and squatted on the ground. Hidden in the shadows, I could not be seen from the street that was illuminated by yellow streetlights. After a few moments, I saw the man stop at the edge of the grass and look toward my direction. He yelled something else in Spanish. I held my breath and felt my heartbeat echo in my ears. My mind was racing, thinking about everything this man might do. To my horror, he started walking in my direction.

I jumped to my feet, slung my pack over my shoulders and hurried through the trees, across a plowed field, and out the other side of the farm. My legs felt like rubber as I hurried, but my fear gave me added strength like I had never felt before. On the other side of the field after crossing a dirt road, my legs gave out, and I collapsed to the ground. I crawled over to a small gully where I lay down flat on my stomach and stared back toward the trees. I felt like I was in the Army,

117

behind enemy lines and evading capture. After a few minutes
of intently watching the dark horizon, I sprawled out on the
ground in exhaustion. I caught my breath and felt my heartbeat return to a normal pace. Eventually I slowly stood up and
continued across the field heading toward the streetlights of
the main road.

Within a few minutes I was along the side of the highway.
In the darkness, I saw the lights of a town on the horizon, and
the sounds of roosters cooing became louder as I approached.
Feeling certain this was Calzada, I quickened my pace. I
wanted to be in the safety of the village as soon as I could.
My legs were tired and still feeling like rubber. Every minute
I kept looking over my shoulder expecting to see the strange
man again. On the gravel path next to the road, I followed
the yellow arrows through a traffic circle, but the path began
drifting away from the lights of the town. I thought perhaps
the route entered town from an unnecessary detour. There was
no reason to think I made a wrong turn because the route was
well marked in this area. Another forty-five minutes passed,
and I was still not in Calzada. I said, to myself, "That's weird.
Maybe the trail just skirted around the town. I guess I'll just
wait until Calzadilla to eat," as my stomach growled.

Around 8:00, up ahead on the road I saw several buildings
on the horizon.

"What? There's no way I walked eight miles that fast."

As I got closer, a sign along the side of the road read Bercianos del Real Camino.

"Bercianos? Where the heck am I?"

I dropped my pack and dug out my guidebook. What I saw
on the map was a split in the Camino just before the town of
Calzada de Coto. I was on an alternative trail that would vastly
increase the mileage to walk and would not reconnect to the
main route for another two days.

"How could I have been so stupid?" I thought to myself.

I considered backtracking an hour to where I missed my

turn, but I was hungry and continued into Bercianos. At the edge of town, I came to a small restaurant with large red shuttered doors. Loud music was resonating from the building. Inside there was a party with about fifty people drinking beer and dancing. A few pilgrims were sitting at a table in the corner, so I sat down with them. I said, over the roar of the crowd to a young man with curly blond hair at the table, "It's kind of early to be partying and drinking, isn't it?"

"Apparently there was a party last night, and it's still going on," he replied. He was sitting with a blond-haired woman, who appeared to be his girlfriend, and a teenage girl with brown hair and a knitted purple hat in the shape of a bear's head. They introduced themselves as being from Poland. I told them of my mistake of walking to the wrong town.

"Right, well, we're heading to El Burgo. I guess your options are to continue to El Burgo or take a taxi to Calzadilla," he said, through a mouthful of food.

My heart was so set on taking a short day and being in Calzadilla that evening, but the idea of taking a taxi felt like it would be cheating.

"Well, maybe you can take a taxi back to Calzada de Coto and pick up where you made the mistake," the man suggested.

Perhaps in hindsight, I should have just accepted the new direction, but since I was so angry at my mistake, the man's suggestion sounded like a good idea. Including the extra bit I walked out of the way, it would still be shorter than continuing on the alternate route to El Burgo. I pushed my way through the party to the counter, ordered a bocadillo jamón, and asked the woman who worked there if she could call a taxi. She said yes, asked where I wanted to go, and made the call.

I ate my bocadillo and chatted with the Polish pilgrims for a few minutes until they continued on their way. After finishing breakfast, I went outside to wait for my taxi. The party was beginning to disperse, and a group of young drunken guys made their way outside. One of the guys, who had a cigarette hanging out of his mouth and was wearing a backwards red baseball cap, asked where I was from and replied with a slurred voice, "I love America! Let me give you a gift," and offered me an empty beer bottle.

"That's alright," I said, and declined his offer.

"You not want my gift," he said, as his tone shifted.

"Nah man, I'm good," I said.

The man then thrust the beer bottle toward me, hitting my chest and nearly knocking me over. A friend from the group came over, put his arm around the man and walked him away. I ducked back inside and waited for the rest of the party to leave.

The two incidents this morning, with unusual locals, had me nervous and shaken. Nothing like this had happened on the entire journey. All I wanted to do was get back onto my planned route and be safe at the albergue. After a few minutes, I went back outside to wait.

The taxi arrived a little after 9:00. The driver, who looked a few years younger than me and had a light shadowy beard, asked where I wanted to go. I showed him Calzada on the guidebook map, and he headed in the direction of the town. The driver had a gourd hanging from his rearview mirror, which was a symbol of the Camino, so I asked him, "Have you ever walked the Camino before?"

He laughed and said, "I tried it once and quit in Pamplona. I do not have what it takes."

"Yeah, it's a tough journey. Don't feel too bad about it."

"Maybe one day I will try again. Or maybe one day I will drive it instead."

The sensation of being in a fast moving car felt surreal. A distance that took me nearly an hour and a half to walk took only a few minutes to drive. I realized these past twenty-four days were probably the longest stretch of time in my life without being in a car. Not until you walk hundreds of miles do you begin to understand distances and how much we take for granted our ability to travel at fast speeds. As I rode in the car, I saw other pilgrims walking along the side of the road and wondered if any of them had accidentally taken the alternate route.

The taxi pulled into the little town of Calzada, and the driver asked where I wanted to get out. I told him anywhere, and he stopped next to a café. I paid him, and he wished me luck. I passed quickly through the dull village and into a barren landscape that continued for six miles. The walk to Calzadilla was over by 12:30, and the first building I came to on the outskirts of town was an albergue called Via Trajana. The two-story red brick building was originally a home that was converted into an albergue. Neatly trimmed hedges and a low metal fence surrounded the building, and a small balcony with potted flowers overlooked a patio.

Inside, a woman with short blond hair and dressed in all white was mopping the floor. She greeted me and called out in Spanish to an older man. He signed me in and led me upstairs to the dorm.

I was assigned to a room with four beds and thankfully no bunks. Two large skylights lit up the area with natural light. The room was larger than usual with each bed having extra blankets and a night stand with a lamp. The cost was about five euros more than most albergues, but it was nice to have a few extra amenities. After a shower, I took a well-deserved nap. All I needed was a restful evening after an incredibly stressful morning.

I was awoken from my afternoon nap by a woman who worked at the albergue as she brought a girl into the room. The girl, with black-framed glasses and long blond hair pulled back into a ponytail, introduced herself as Mila from Germany. She was eighteen years old but looked much younger. Mila had graduated from high school that past spring and was taking a gap year. I immediately felt concerned that she was on the Camino alone and suddenly understood why my parents and others in my life were worried about me. I thought, "Man, she's just a kid out here all on her own. But I guess I'm not that much older."

Mila and I talked about our plans for the following day where there would be an eleven-mile stretch with no towns or services during the fifteen-mile walk to Mansilla de las Mulas. We would have to carry extra food for breakfast. Once Mila was settled in, we both ventured into town to find a supermarket. Despite being a small town, the streets were confusing. Most of the buildings were built with the same red brick design, making every street look similar. The supermarket was just a house with a handwritten sign that simply said "SHOP" on the door. Feeling slightly nervous, I knocked on the locked door of the faded white building. Mila stepped back several feet behind me when we heard a commotion of locks being undone. The door opened inwards with a hard thrust, and a short chubby bald man with features similar to the American actor Danny DeVito greeted us. He blurted something in Spanish with a wide smile, but I said, "Hablamos Ingles."

"Ah, okay. Come in, Come in."

Mila and I walked into a dark hallway with chipped blue-tiled floor and cracked walls and were led into a small cramped room with a flickering fluorescent light on the ceiling. All four walls had shelves of food ranging from produce to bags of flour and boxes of cereal. The man kept pointing to and holding up different items repeatedly saying, "Do you want this? How about this? Or maybe this?" We picked out bananas and some packages of cookies, paid, and immediately exited.

"That was a dodgy place, yeah?" Mila asked, on our walk back.

"Yeah. Is that the supermarket for the entire town?"

"Probably. I think most of these villages are very poor and do not have many conveniences."

The Halfway Mark

Shortly after we returned to the room, two more women arrived. They introduced themselves as Josephine from Germany and Susan from Seattle, Washington. Both Josephine and Susan knew Mila from previous albergues. Josephine was an older woman with short curly brown hair and stocky broad shoulders. Susan was slim with medium-length blond hair and looked to be in her early fifties but had a youthful face with a clear complexion and no wrinkles. All three of my roommates were friendly, and I was glad I decided to stay the night in Calzadilla. Josephine and Mila talked in German to each other for a while, and I talked with Susan about how nice it was to meet another American. I told her that I had muscular dystrophy, and she said, "That's good that you are out here walking the Camino. It's nice to see someone who actually has a purpose for being out here."

I thought for a while about what Susan said about having a purpose on the Camino. Several people mentioned that before, but what was my purpose? Having muscular dystrophy was not a purpose, and proving something was not my purpose. My purpose was to reach Santiago. Maybe this comment was not about me but about her. Perhaps Susan was struggling to discover her own reason for being on the trail, and seeing me with an added burden made it seem like I had everything figured out. In reality, I had nothing figured out, and my purpose was no clearer from any other pilgrim.

While everyone was resting, Mila asked Susan, "Can Bryan join us for dinner tonight?"

Susan smiled, turned to me and asked, "Would you like to have dinner with us tonight?"

"Sure! I don't have any other plans."

At 7:00, we went downstairs to the dining room and were joined by an Australian brother and sister in their thirties named Levi and Zoe, who everyone already knew. Both had kind smiles and dark complexions. Levi was tall with a large build, while Zoe was a stocky woman with long hair. With all

123

My Own Pace

six of us at the same table, the conversation was very lively and fun. I ordered pasta with meat sauce, grilled pork loin, and ice cream for dessert. Endless bottles of wine graced the table, adding to the energy. Everyone told their stories from the day, but I remained mostly quiet since I was still not familiar with the group. After a brief break in conversation, Zoe said, "So Bryan, since you're the new one, we all get to pick on you tonight."

I opened up a bit about my background and my experience so far, and the conversation shifted to me explaining how I managed the entire Camino with no blisters. With mention of this fact, Levi joked, "Get up and get out of here. You're not one of us if you don't have blisters."

As we talked further, and I mentioned my Camino began a week before everyone else, Zoe asked, "So have you been spending extra time in all of the towns?"

"I have muscular dystrophy, so I walk shorter distances each day and take my time," I said.

"You have muscular dystrophy, and you are hiking the Camino?" she asked inquisitively.

"Yeah, it's been an adventure making it this far," I said.

"I'll drink to that!" Zoe responded, as she poured everyone more wine.

Levi said, "Well, I take that back about you not being one of us. Blisters are nothing compared to what you probably have to deal with. Welcome to the family."

Zoe raised her glass and said, "To a Buen Caminio."

"Buen Camino," we all cheered, as we clinked our glasses.

During the meal, we all agreed to sleep at the same albergue the next day in Mansilla de las Mulas, so Mila called ahead and reserved six beds for everyone. Feeling part of a "Camino family" again was nice after several days of being mostly alone. Though I was beginning to enjoy moving at my own pace, being connected with a group gave me some added

124

security. Even if you have a bad day, there is someone to talk to and boost your spirits. After three glasses of wine, everyone starts to feel like family. I went to the bathroom midway through the meal, and I came back to find my recently emptied wine glass full again.

"I thought I finished this glass."

"Well, they give us this wine because we're supposed to finish it. You ain't gonna do that with an empty glass," Zoe said.

Just as we finished the last bottle and Zoe said, "Mission accomplished," the waitress brought over two more.

"We've got work to do," Levi said.

Susan, Mila, and Josephine slowly backed out of what was becoming competitive drinking, and I finished the last of the wine with Zoe and Levi. As we started laughing at every incomprehensible sound that came out of our mouths, a voice in the back of my head said, "You're going to have a hangover from hell tomorrow morning."

Being over the halfway mark, I figured one drunken night would be acceptable. I walked over two hundred sixty miles; a headache would not slow me down now. After we finished our meal, we all staggered back upstairs to our beds, and Zoe said, "Bryan, don't take this the wrong way, but we are all walking up the stairs like you right now."

Sleep came easily that night, but waking up the next morning proved difficult. The night before, Josephine gave me an aspirin to take in the morning. After throwing my gear together and swallowing the pill, I was out the door by 5:30. This fifteen-mile day was going to be my longest on the Camino. I had a terrifying fear of making another wrong turn after my debacle yesterday, so I checked the guidebook frequently to identify landmarks along the way.

The entire day I hardly saw any other pilgrims on the trail. I found it funny how some days the trail would be packed with pilgrims, while other days I felt completely alone. In the

Meseta, the barren landscape lacks many landmarks, so the loneliness is much more obvious.

I arrived in Mansilla around 1:30 that afternoon. Seeing the town after walking fifteen miles gave me an intense feeling of triumph. Tomorrow I would be in León, the last major city, along the scale of Burgos and Pamplona, that I would pass through before Santiago. Just under two hundred eighty miles were behind me.

The albergue Mila had booked for us was called El Jardín del Camino and was right at the entrance to town. It was a two-story brick building surrounded with adobe walls that were covered with ivy, and a closed-in green lawn with tables and chairs. I knocked on a sliding green metal gate that immediately rolled open. A man in his mid-fifties with a scruffy beard greeted me with a firm handshake. I assumed he was the owner. Two young women around my age with dark brown hair, who were the daughters of the owner, led me inside across the lawn into the albergue.

When we walked into the café area slightly illuminated from outside light, one of the women explained there was limited staff today because of a party in town. No food was being served that evening, so I would have to find a café for dinner. After being checked in, I was directed up a flight of steps into a large open dorm area with polished floors, yellow walls, and fifteen bunks. I was the first pilgrim to arrive, which was not surprising based on how few pilgrims I saw throughout the day. After settling in, I showered and then lay down in bed and waited for the others from last night to arrive.

Mila and Josephine strolled in first and took beds near me. Susan, Levi, and Zoe arrived a few minutes later.

Zoe said, "I thought you said you walked slowly? You're here way before any of us."

"What time did you leave this morning?" I asked.

"8:30. You?" Zoe asked.

"5:30," I laughed.

The Halfway Mark

As everyone talked about their day and how they managed the fifteen miles with little amenities, more pilgrims began to trickle in. Our group went outside to the courtyard to unwind and Zoe bought beers for everyone.

"More drinks after last night?" I said, as Zoe placed a tray of six tall beers on the table.

"Have you learned nothing on the Camino? This is what you do every night, drink!"

"The peer pressure is real," I said, and took a sip of beer.

While we were all relaxing and chatting, we talked about reaching the city of León tomorrow. Everyone had different plans, so we all would not be together in León. Zoe, Levi, and Mila were walking beyond the city to the next town, Susan was getting a private hotel room, and Josephine was taking a bus to the city for a rest day. Their group had been together for almost a week, and they all seemed disappointed to be separating. I felt sad as well, since I was getting used to seeing the same people at the end of each day again. This reminded me of how sad I felt when I parted from Alma and Beth, but at this point the comings and goings of people was commonplace.

After hanging out for a while, I decided to venture farther into town to find a restaurant for a more substantial meal. Levi and Susan decided to take a nap, and Mila and Zoe were going to the supermarket to stock up on some items. Mila asked if I needed anything, so I asked for a new stick of deodorant. There were many comforts I went without, but I did not want to offend others with a body odor that was easy to prevent.

The town was eerily empty as I walked to a restaurant recommended by one of the girls who worked at the albergue. Loud music echoed several blocks away, and I assumed this was the party everyone in the town was attending. Though it only had a population of just under two thousand, Mansilla was much larger than I expected, with most of its brick style buildings packed closely together. The dusty adobe homes of the Meseta were mostly absent now that I was nearing a large city and close to a major terrain change. I found a small family-owned restaurant with outdoor seating in a gated courtyard. The middle-aged owner took my order as his young daughter ran around the courtyard bouncing a little red ball. As the only customer, my meal of pasta, roast chicken, and of course, ice cream for dessert, was brought out quickly.

Susan had just awoken from a nap when I returned from the restaurant and was hungry for dinner, so I recommended the restaurant where I had eaten. I paid Mila for the deodorant, got ready for bed, and was asleep before 8:00. The night was generally quiet since the albergue was not even half full. Unfortunately I did not get a chance to say goodbye to Susan or Mila, and all the others from the past two days. Everyone was still asleep when I left at 5:30 the next morning. I would never see them again on the Camino.

The scenery on the trail became increasingly industrial on the morning I left Mansilla and traveled into the outskirts of León. Much of what I read about this city highlighted its nice vibes, but I was feeling none of them. Through the city, crammed with cars and crowded streets, my mind began to vibrate from sensory overload. Perhaps so many days in the Meseta had poisoned my brain. Everything seemed too loud and moved too fast. I kept my hands deep in my pockets, constantly checking my wallet every time a group of people passed. For reasons I cannot properly explain, I wanted to be somewhere else, far away from people. Everyone I passed seemed hostile and made me feel uneasy. "I hate cities. What am I doing here?" I asked myself. My thoughts were focused on finding the albergue, getting a good night sleep, and slipping out of the city during the quiet morning. I had heard good things about León, but my mind was not in the right place to explore.

After navigating a maze of streets and intersections surrounded by old stone and brick buildings, I found the albergue on a side street, tucked away from the tourist-ridden shops. I spent the rest of the day at the albergue and a small cafe across the street. Exploring cities was never something I enjoyed doing alone, and I wished I was with a group of people that I knew. Despite finding myself in a funk that day, I thought about how big of an accomplishment it was making it to León, the last major milestone in the Meseta before its official ending in Astorga, still a few days away. León was farther than I ever could have imagined walking when I had started my journey, but the distant mountains were now only three days away, acting as the final defensive walls to breach before reaching Santiago. I was closing in on my goal, yet it still felt as distant as ever. Twenty-six days and two hundred ninety miles were behind me. The snoring in the albergue that night was louder than ever before, but I eventually fell asleep thanks to my earplugs wedged tightly in place.

My last few days in the Meseta breezed by, until finally, on September 15, I crossed a bridge over the Tuerto River in Astorga where several locals were fishing. Geographically, this was where the Meseta came to an end. For twelve days and nearly one hundred fifty miles, my life had been defined by this flat, featureless landscape. The lack of physical challenges was about to end. One hundred seventy-five miles remained until Santiago, through a route that was dominated by the Galician mountains, known for its lush forests and unpredictable rain.

Beyond the bridge, past cornfields and an abandoned warehouse covered with graffiti, a group of two men and a woman caught up to me, and we exchanged a "Buen Camino." One man who was in his early fifties, with receding dark hair, prominent nose, and glasses, turned abruptly and asked, "Where are you from?"

I told him New Jersey, and he replied, "I'll be damned, me too! Where in New Jersey?"

"Trenton. You?"

"Mount Laurel."

My Own Pace

"Wow, that's only about forty minutes away!"

"I'm originally from Brooklyn, but I've been living in Mount Laurel with my family for many years."

"Well, you're officially the closest person to home I've met."

"I'm Logan by the way," he said, as he reached out with a firm handshake. His group was moving at a faster pace than me, and he slowly began inching ahead.

A half hour later as I passed through the town square, I heard a voice with a Brooklyn accent call out my name from across the square, and I saw Logan sitting at a table with his two companions eating lunch.

I took a seat with them and was formally introduced to the group, a Korean woman named Jae and a young Italian guy with curly brown hair named Anthony. Jae began her Camino in Burgos, Anthony in León, and Logan, who had previously walked the entire Camino in 2013 with his wife, started in St-Jean. As everyone ate their bocadillos and various tapas snacks, I pulled out a couple granola bars to munch on. Logan's group was stopping in Astorga for the day, so I wished them well after a few minutes of chatting and continued on. My destination, Murias, was just three miles away.

At the albergue that evening I spent some time writing in my journal and finally finished reading *Man's Search for Meaning*. Now I had to fulfill my promise to George, who gave me the book, and find the right pilgrim to pass it on to. As I sat outside that evening, there was a growing cool breeze and a drop in temperature due to the elevation change. The trail through the coming mountains would include the highest point on the Camino, at nearly five thousand feet. Though the climb would be more gradual than the Pyrenees, the increase was still significant since I was currently around three thousand feet.

The temperature in Murias was below freezing when I woke up. I survived the night in the unheated room with the

130

extra blankets left on the beds by the staff. Not wanting to be exposed to the morning cold for too long, I opted to wait an extra half hour before I hit the trail around 6:00 a.m., bundled in all the clothing I had.

My destination that day was unknown, since I was unsure how much ground I could cover in the increasingly mountainous landscape. I was either walking nine miles to Rabanal del Camino, midway up the climb, or thirteen miles to Foncebadón, just over a mile before the high point. The gravelly trail out of Murias started as a gradual incline and was not too taxing on my legs. As I moved farther away from the light pollution of Astorga, there was a clear view of the stars, and the prominent belt of the Milky Way appeared to be pointing the way to Santiago.

Long before the Camino was a Catholic pilgrimage, the same route was followed by ancient Celts who followed the Milky Way, across the Iberian Peninsula to Cape Finisterre, to what they believed was the true end of the world. In Latin, "finis terrae" directly translates to "end of the earth." Being on this path created a feeling of connection to ancient humans who had been heading west for as long as recorded history. Many pilgrims who walk to Santiago continue for several more days to Finisterre to reach the Atlantic Ocean. I was still undecided if that portion of the trail would be included in my journey. Due to time constraints, my walk would most likely end in Santiago as planned, but I would make a decision when the time came.

The first three miles of the day to Santa Catalina de Somoza was rocky and followed alongside a rarely used dirt road with overgrown grass and shrubs. At the edge of the village, as the sun began to rise, I tripped on a loose rock, causing another near ankle sprain, but luckily I was able to catch myself. Those few seconds after a fall are always terrifying, as I quickly check for any injuries and walk a few steps to make sure everything is working properly. Even with a headlamp, seeing obstructions on the trail was difficult, and shadows caused the ground to look uneven. With the assurance that I had no breaks or sprains, I continued into the village to find a café for breakfast, but nothing was open. Besides a few homes, the majority of the settlement was abandoned buildings. The structures were built of flat stones with any mortar having crumbled away long ago. Some of the foundations were covered in ivy and still had wooden doors slowly rotting away. Small trees and bushes grew out of broken windows and through sections of missing roofs.

Disappointed by not finding an open café for breakfast, I ate a granola bar as I walked. On the way out of town, an American couple from Ohio, named John and Cheryl, began walking with me. John was tall with a bald head, a dark beard, and wearing shorts that exposed long hairy legs. His choice of clothing seemed unusual for the cold morning. I initially thought his wife was his daughter. She was almost a foot shorter, and her face and blond hair were mostly hidden by a hood. After we began talking, I could tell they were both in their mid-fifties. They began in St-Jean the week after me and were staying in Foncebadón tonight. Learning that I started long before them prompted the usual questions, so I explained my situation. John thought it was brave of me to walk the Camino, but what amazed him more was the fact that I was surviving on less than thirty euros a day.

"Cheryl and I struggle to stay below sixty euros a day each."

"Well, I stayed in albergues the entire time, never stayed in a hotel, and I always order the cheapest things on menus and don't drink coffee every morning."

"Yeah, the coffee does add up quick for us," John said, with a chuckle.

"I bet. I've never been a big spender, so that seems to translate to my Camino."

Eventually John said, "Well, Bryan, I think Cheryl and I

are going to move on ahead of you here, but you've been great company. I wish you the best."

The walk to the next town, El Ganso, was quiet, and I did not see another pilgrim the entire time. By beginning my day several miles outside Astorga, most of the crowds were still behind me. El Ganso, meaning "goose" in Spanish, was smaller than Santa Catalina but also filled with ruins and crumbling structures. The paved road out of town began to rise in elevation, and the mountains became more prominent on the horizon. A row of wind turbines graced the top of the nearby ridge as I passed through a hilly area with fields of dry grasses and an occasional thorny bush.

Slightly past the town, I saw two legs in long grey pants sticking out of a patch of grass. My first thought was that a pilgrim was taking a nap. A sleeping pilgrim was not unusual to see along the trail, but the shoes on the body were not hiking shoes. The legs were stiff with no movement. As I slowly approached, I saw it was an older man. He had a narrow face, pale skin, a short trimmed beard, and his arms were motionless.

"Hola?" I said.

The body lay still.

"Hello? Are you alright?" I said, a little louder as I saw no movement.

I inched closer, and I did not notice any breathing. I tapped his leg with my hiking pole, but he did not move.

"Oh my God! He's dead! He's dead! This man is dead!" I exclaimed.

I looked up and down the trail and saw nobody. Yelling for help was useless. The body was positioned in the grass in a way that it could have gone unnoticed all morning. John and Cheryl were probably the only other pilgrims to pass by here today. My hands trembled as I took out my phone to call the police. After my phone powered on I saw I had no cell service. I stood there for a few moments staring and wondering what had happened. Suddenly I saw his arm twitch, and his head rolled slowly to the right.

"Hey! Are you okay?"

His eyes opened, and he raised his hand to give me a thumbs up. As he moved I saw a whiskey bottle beside him. He was drunk.

"Okay. Si, okay. Thank you," he said, in broken English and a slurred voice.

With a slight struggle he formed his mouth into a smile suggesting he understood I thought he was dead. I could tell he would be okay. He probably drank himself into a stupor last night and was just waking up now. With a slight laugh, I bid the man farewell and continued walking. I looked back over my shoulder a minute later and saw the man standing upright, making his way back towards El Ganso. I wondered if he was homeless, or had a wife at home waiting to give him hell. Either way, this was probably a regular occurrence for him.

A few minutes after I passed the drunk man, the tendon behind my right knee started to hurt, but this time the steep terrain did not allow me to adjust my stride. Slowly, I limped up the hill feeling disheartened. My pace was cut in half, and every step was agony. I had enough to worry about, and now I had to deal with this. When I crossed the Pyrenees, I was fresh, but for these mountains, I was worn down from thirty days on the Camino. My optimism was still strong, but the feeling that my spirit might break was growing. I wondered if I could hold up. The thought of having to cross more mountains seemed an impossible task.

9

CARRYING MY BURDEN

As I struggled up the hill to the town of Rabanal, with continued tendon pain in my right knee, I heard a man's voice with a Brooklyn accent call out, "Bryan! My man!" and I turned around to see a familiar New Jerseyite, Logan.

"Hey, how are ya!" I said.

"I'm doing alright, but how are you?" Logan asked, as he looked down at my legs.

"My knees and feet hurt, but I'm hanging in there," I said.

"Sorry to hear that, my man. Where are you walking to today?"

"I planned on Foncebadón, but I'm not sure if that will happen now."

"Yeah, maybe that's not such a good idea. I'm stopping in Rabanal. If you stop there, I'll buy you a beer."

"Sounds good, maybe I'll see you up there then," I said, as he moved on past me.

"Yup, I'll see you there."

A half hour after Logan passed, I stumbled into the outskirts of Rabanal and stopped at the first albergue I found, called La Senda. After I checked in, I stopped in a café next door for lunch before I took a long nap. I awoke at 6:30 p.m. to find most of the beds occupied, and the sound of Logan's booming voice coming from outside the window.

135

I found Logan with a Dutch guy, Eugene, who I knew from my albergue the night before, both drinking beers at one of several tables in front of the café.

"Hey, Bryan! Can I still buy you a beer?"

"Sure," I said, as I sat down with them.

Logan went inside the café and quickly returned with a half liter of beer and a bowl of chips, and I bought another bocadillo jamón. I tried to repay Logan, but he put his hand up and said, "Next time I see you, you can buy me one."

Logan went on to talk about his previous time hiking the entire Camino and comparing it to the Appalachian Trail in the United States. His son hiked the trail several years ago, and Logan had hiked a portion with him.

"There's much more freedom on the American trails in regards to sleeping and camping, but you don't have all the huts and albergues like they have in Europe," Logan said.

"Yeah, I would prefer camping over albergues just to get away from the snoring," I joked.

"But I think that's what makes the Camino something unique. You're dealing more with people, you're dealing with snoring, and sometimes it's better to be doing the things you don't prefer. We grow when we are challenged, and people have a way of challenging us," Logan said.

"That's a good point. It's definitely been a challenge out here," I said, as I took a sip of beer.

"But the Camino is more spiritual than the Appalachian Trail. You can feel it. It's a path that has been walked for nearly a millennium, and we're all a part of that story," Logan said.

"Did you bring a rock to leave behind at Cruz de Ferro tomorrow?" I asked.

I was referring to the place on the trail, where pilgrims leave behind a rock which represents letting go of a burden carried from home.

Logan replied, "You know, actually I didn't bring one. My

wife and I did that when we walked the Way in 2013. It just felt like more of a one-time deal, but it's definitely a spiritual experience. Did you bring a rock?"

"Yeah, I did, but I still need to decide what burden I will leave behind with the rock."

"I don't think it has to be a burden. It can represent anything you want. It doesn't have to be religious. The Camino is a personal journey and doesn't have to be defined by anything," Logan said.

"That's something I've thought about a lot on the Camino. I'm not really a Catholic and have been struggling to understand how to define what I really believe. I'm not sure what God is or if I'm an atheist," I said, taking another sip of beer.

"I was raised Catholic but don't practice anymore. Maybe I'm a bit of a nihilist, but when a philosophy, or any religion, be it the Catholic Church or anything, becomes institutionalized, it loses its meaning," Logan said.

"That's really a true point. But what about something like transcendentalism that rejects institutions over the individual?"

Logan laughed and said, "Even Thoreau and Emerson had ideas they wanted to slap a label on. I believe in the good of people, though I don't believe that needs to be defined by an "-ism" or a steeple over a building, even if the basis of the idea is about the good of people."

Logan paused for a moment and said, "Let me show you this," and rolled up his right sleeve to reveal a tattoo of Jesus wearing a crown of thorns in front of a cross. The drops of blood dripping from his head were colored in red. He continued to say, "People are always confused by my tattoo of Jesus when I talk about not having a religion. But Jesus had one main idea, to love each other. That's why I have this. Not because of Christianity, but to remind me that we're all human and we all suffer," Logan said.

After Logan revealed his tattoo, he glanced at his watch

and left the table abruptly. He had made a promise to another pilgrim to attend a prayer service with them. "I'm a man of my word, for better or for worse. I'll see you on the trail again soon."

That was the last time I saw Logan on the Camino. After he left, I talked to Eugene as he lit up a joint to smoke and finished his beer. I smelled a faint hint of weed mixed into his tobacco.

"I know. I know. It's very stereotypical of me to be smoking weed since I'm Dutch. They don't care in Spain anyway," he said, as a puff of smoke came from his mouth, and he gestured with his joint toward others walking by on the street.

Eugene started his Camino in Geneva, Switzerland, and noted how different the Camino is if started before St-Jean. He had been using his tent the entire way, camping in the mountains and in farm fields. Rabanal had a campground where Eugene was staying.

As our conversation became deeper, I said, "I don't know how I'm going to explain all this to people when I return home."

"You can't really explain this to someone who hasn't experienced it. You'll tell a story here, show a picture there, but it will never be the same," he said.

"It's just that the Camino changed me in ways I can't explain. It showed me that anything is possible. I never thought I would make it this far," I said.

"But you did. You made it. No one can ever take it away from you. You hike the Camino for yourself. You don't have to be able to explain it," he said.

"My thoughts seem to keep drifting toward explaining this to others as I near the end. I'm starting to think about my flight home and going back to work," I said.

Eugene laughed and said, "Don't think about it. Live in the now. As soon as you start thinking about the future, you stop living in the moment. You're here on the Camino probably one time in your life, so make sure you are here and not somewhere else. Once you get to Santiago, you can think about the return journey."

Sitting there, I began to feel cold, a sign I was heading into higher elevations. I finished my beer, said goodbye to Eugene, and headed back to the albergue. I realized that Eugene and Logan were some of the few people that I connected with but never told about my muscular dystrophy. At that point in the Camino I was tired of hearing over and over, "you're an inspiration" or "you're a hero." Although the Camino made me more open to sharing facts about my life with others, sometimes it felt good to not have someone know and feel like my struggles on the Camino were not any different from everyone else. I knew there would be a time in the future when people would see my condition immediately, but I was not there yet. I was living in the present. As I walked back from the café, I saw a tall man in his mid-sixties with thick grey hair.

"Connor!" I called out. This was the man from Florida I met in Uterga and last saw in Azofra eighteen days ago, the night of my food poisoning. I remembered the story I heard about his daughter dying several years before and how he and his wife Evelyn were walking to mourn. Connor was not aware I knew of this story.

Connor and I talked for a few minutes about everything that had happened since we last saw each other. He and Evelyn were having some foot pain that slowed down their pace. They were planning to take a shorter ten-mile day tomorrow to the town of El Acebo. I was tentatively thinking about stopping there as well, so we said goodbye knowing we would probably see each other again soon. Meeting people like Connor whom I last saw so long ago always created a warm feeling. I often reflected on people I met throughout my journey and wondered where they were. Most people I never expected to see again, which made running into them more exciting. No matter how much slower or faster you walk than another person, your paths are never that far apart. Connor would not be the last person to make a miraculous reappearance on my Camino.

I slept well that night even though the temperature was near freezing, and once again I put on every bit of clothing I had. Tomorrow would be a difficult walk up to Cruz de Ferro. At just under five miles into my day, I would reach a place I had anticipated since my journey began, when I felt my journey was doomed. Remembering what Logan had said about Cruz de Ferro being whatever I wanted it to be made me even more uncertain about what tomorrow would bring. Along with this, tomorrow would pose the greatest elevation change since my first days. I felt that the tendon pain was my body warning me to slow down and be careful. I was still confident, but there was a growing feeling deep inside me that something bad was lingering ahead of me on the trail.

I was up early the next morning but once again on the trail a little later than usual to limit my time in the cold before sunrise. I had forgotten to bring gloves or mittens but remembered I had a pair of wool socks that worked just as well. I probably looked ridiculous wearing them on my hands, but they were warm. The beginning of the route was difficult in the dark through a forest. Eventually the trail spilled out onto a steep, winding, narrow road. If a car came around one of the bends, I would not be visible and could be hit. Luckily the time was much too early for most Spaniards to be on the road. I kept hoping for a wide shoulder to appear, but it never did. Quickening my pace, I hoped to get off the road as soon as possible. After a few hundred feet I had not seen any yellow trail markers but assumed they were just not visible in the dark.

Eventually I saw a pair of headlamps from people coming up behind me. The sight made me feel confident because I was no longer alone, but a few minutes later the lights disappeared. Feeling confused, I took off my pack and checked the map in my guidebook and realized the trail was along the side of the road and not on it. As I stood there quietly, I heard voices below me down a steep drop off. Those must be the people who were behind me. I had gone the wrong way again! I stomped my foot on the ground and grunted as I put my pack back on and trudged back down the steep road. Not only was I aggravated that I made another wrong turn, but I put so much energy into tackling that hill when I still had a difficult climb ahead of me. Even though I only walked fifteen minutes out of my way, it felt like so much more when it was all unnecessary steps. Backtracking to the place where the Camino spilled onto the main road, I saw that the trail crossed over the road and did not continue on it. Even with my headlamp on, it was easy to miss a turn.

Back on the correct path, I was confronted with a seemingly endless path of jagged rocks scattered along the narrow dirt trail. Having to step from rock to rock in the dark and chance a fall with my shaky legs was not worth the risk. I imagined the voices of so many of my friends and family telling me to sit down and wait for more daylight. A low dirt embankment along the left side of the trail seemed like an adequate location, so I sat down to wait for sunrise, which did not arrive until 7:30. Several people passed and were startled to find me sitting there in the dark. I pretended to be rummaging through my pack or drinking water every time I heard a voice or saw an approaching headlamp. I did not want to appear injured or out of place.

After the sun rose, I continued walking. The trail was still rocky but it had a gradual incline across a landscape cluttered with trees, tall grasses, and a view of rolling mountains to the south. There was a steep hill that butted up against a road crossing with a flight of a dozen cement steps with no handrail. I paused at the base of the steps and wondered how I would get up them. There was no way I could wear my pack up the steps without my legs giving out. Even the smooth dirt area next to the steps was too steep for me.

My Own Pace

I turned around to see if there was anyone who could help me, but I was alone. After thinking for a moment, I took off my pack, got down on my hands and knees, and dragged my pack up the hill next to the steps. My body strained as I struggled to dig in my feet, push myself up, and not let go of my pack while my hands grabbed onto clumps of grass for added support. Once I reached the top, I brushed the dirt off my shirt and pants, and put my pack back on.

After I crossed the road, a woman with a French accent approached from behind and exclaimed, "Did you fall? Are you okay?"

I turned around to see a couple slightly older than me with concerned expressions. The tall woman, with blond hair pulled back under a red headband was wearing a blue flannel shirt. The guy was taller, with curly black hair, a prominent nose, and dressed in a white t-shirt and hiking pants.

"No, I'm okay," I said.

"But your pack is so filthy," the woman said.

"Oh, yeah, I had to crawl and drag my pack up the hill back there."

"What? You crawled and dragged? Why?"

"I have a condition with my muscles called muscular dystrophy. I have trouble walking up hills and steps."

The woman paused for a minute and said something to the guy in French. His face lit up and his jaw dropped as he walked over and gave me a hug.

"I told him what you told me, and he says you are his hero," the woman said.

"Can I take a picture with you?" the guy asked.

"Sure," I said, as he handed a camera to the woman, and she took our picture.

"What is your name?" the woman asked.

"Bryan," I said.

"I am Renee, and this is Louis," she said, as they shook my hand.

Carrying My Burden

They began walking with me, and Renee explained that she was from France and Louis was from Quebec. Both of them began their Camino in the middle of the Meseta and were even more amazed when I told them I began in St-Jean.

Louis said, "Your strength is true. Do not let go of your strength," as he patted me on the back.

As they finally moved on, Renee said, "You are my hero too, Bryan."

Shortly after Louis and Renee passed, the trail became steeper and turned into a rocky ditch that caused me to fall hard and hit my knee on a rock. I rolled over and moaned with pain, but I was able to get back up, only to fall a few steps later and hit the same knee. I stood up and kicked my backpack as hard as I could and threw my hiking pole on the ground. My heart pounded, and the same few sentences kept running through my head. "What am I doing here? I'm tired of falling! Why do I have to have muscular dystrophy? Why did I come to the Camino?"

As I picked up my things and continued walking, the dark thoughts continued to spiral in my head. "Oh, you're such a hero, Bryan. You're so brave. Well, maybe I don't want to be a hero! Maybe it's all a lie! What is any of this really proving except it's really hard for me! Maybe it's time for the hero to GIVE UP!"

Tears began to roll down my cheek as I kept struggling over the rocks. There was a smooth, narrow path on each side of the ditch, but I knew a fall up there would be much worse than falling here. A few bruises and scrapes were preferable to a broken leg. Surely I looked ridiculous picking the difficult path, but it was the safer path for me.

My validation of how strange I looked came when an old man with a bald head, grey beard, and wearing a black long sleeve shirt, passed me and said in an Irish accent, "It looks like you are having some trouble. Perhaps you should walk up here rather than down on the rocks."

My Own Pace

I wiped my tears and said, "Yeah, well, I have muscular dystrophy, and I fall a lot, so I don't want to fall from up there."

"Oh, I am so sorry. You know your body better than me. I am sorry," he said.

Moments later I tripped and fell again, banging my knees once more on a hard rock. I let out an annoyed groan as I struggled to stand. The man jumped down into the ditch to help.

"Are you okay?" he asked.

"I'm fine," I said, as I began to walk away.

"But you are crying and your face is all red. Please sit and rest for a moment."

Resisting the urge to push past the old man and avoid hearing another person tell me how wonderful I was, I sat down on the embankment next to the ditch. Maybe this man came into my journey for a reason. He sat down next to me, pulled out a canteen and took a swig. He gestured toward me and said, "You should drink some water. It's important to stay hydrated."

As I took my water bottle out and took a few sips, we briefly introduced ourselves. His name was Father Cornelius.

"You're a priest?" I asked.

"Yes, I am."

"Most religious officials I've encountered on the trail were with a group and never alone." I said.

Cornelius laughed and said, "No one is really ever alone on the Camino. God is always with us in times of need. We just have to listen for him, and he speaks to us."

"It's funny how things happen when they do. For the past few hours I've been feeling more down than I've felt since my first days on the trail, and then you came along."

"Are you a Catholic?"

"I was raised Catholic, but I am no longer a Catholic."

"Even if we lose God for a while or have never known

him, the Camino is a place where we can find his love. Jesus
was once a pilgrim of faith on a mission of discovery too. To
be on the Way is to be in the company of Jesus."

After Father Cornelius's talk of God, we sat quietly and
did not say much more to each other. I understood it was his
duty to spread the word of God but was humbled by his mod-
esty. This was the first priest I spoke with on my journey, and
it could not have come at a better time. After a few minutes,
a feeling of bliss came over me. I wondered, if God could
take on a human form and walk among us, would he do it as
a priest?

Once I felt ready to continue, we walked slowly through
the rocks until the path became smooth but still very steep as
a light fog began to roll in through a thick wall of trees. After
a few minutes, he said, "Well, Bryan, you seem to be in better
spirits now, so I will move ahead. Maybe I will see you again
later today."

The incline caused the tendons behind my right knee to
hurt again as I slowly limped up. At the top, the trees cleared
and a strong wind whipped through the open landscape.
Though the climb was steep, the increase was so gradual that
I did not realize how high I had climbed. Up ahead, the stone
buildings of Foncebadón came into view. The majority of the
town was crumbling stone ruins with trees growing out of collapsed roofs. The main road was completely washed out with
rocks poking out of the ground. Some sections were so rocky
that my feet slid beneath me. I stopped in a café for a quick
breakfast before I continued onward.

The number of pilgrims on the trail increased around Foncebadón. This was a popular location for starting and stopping
each day, due to its closeness to Cruz de Ferro. Just over a
mile out of town, in front of a backdrop of a clear blue sky, the
monument appeared on the horizon. About twenty pilgrims
were gathered around the massive pile of rocks surrounding the iron cross affixed atop a wooden pole about ten feet

tall. As I made my way closer, my thoughts shifted towards the burden I needed to leave behind. What was my burden? I paused for a moment and removed a reddish rock from my pocket and held it in my open palm.

A voice came to me from four years earlier, in July 2013. The words vividly burned into my mind:

"You've got real grit," my uncle Jeb said, as he helped me up, and I brushed the dirt off my knees after another fall. Looming another mile and a half away was our goal, the rocky summit of Medicine Bow Peak. High above the timberline there were no trees to obscure the constant reminder of how far we still had to climb. The mountain stands at an elevation of 12,018 feet and is a four mile hike from base to summit, making it the highest point in southern Wyoming.

"I'm gonna make it," I said, looking back at Jeb who was patiently following me up the mountainside.

"Long as those dark clouds keep their distance," Jeb said, as he adjusted his black cowboy hat and pointed westward.

The brilliant blue sky was giving way to several dark clouds on the horizon, and we pushed forward hoping to avoid a possible thunderstorm. Our rate of ascent slowed as the trail became steeper, and my legs felt heavier. I used a hiking pole for balance and sometimes pushed off of boulders with my hands. After a series of rocky switchbacks, the trail led across a deep snow patch next to a drop off of several hundred feet. One slip here would send me sliding down the mountain. Uncle Jeb took a climbing harness out of his pack for me to wear and attached a rope from it to himself. After inching through the packed snow, with several falls that only resulted in laughter and cold hands, we came to a boulder field leading to the summit. With shaky legs, I cautiously stepped from boulder to boulder until I was standing next to a splintering wooden pole supported by a pile of rocks marking the top of the mountain.

"Congrats, you did it. Happy Birthday!" Jeb said.

Carrying My Burden

At twenty years old, I accomplished my most difficult physical challenge to date. What would have taken the average hiker an hour and a half took me almost three hours.

Standing on the summit, I closed my eyes, took a deep breath of fresh alpine air, and listened to the wind rush past my ears. From here, the view was a seemingly endless expanse of mountains known as the Snowy Range. Several lakes at the base of the mountain mirrored the blue sky and clouds. Before heading down the mountain, I picked up a small reddish rock near the summit marker. This rock would be a reminder that I had the "grit" to accomplish whatever goals I set my mind on.

On the drive back to the town of Encampment, I held the rock from Medicine Bow Peak and rubbed my fingers over the smooth edges. No one but me could understand the amount of endurance needed to pick up this rock.

My uncle Jeb was originally from New Jersey, where I lived, but settled in Wyoming in the early 1970s after dropping out of college and hitch-hiking around the United States for several years. After coming to Wyoming, he worked on a cattle ranch and lived in a tiny cabin in the mountains. As a child, several of my family's vacations brought us through Wyoming to visit Jeb. In the summer of 2013, after my first year of college, I was living in Wyoming and working at the dining hall of a ritzy dude ranch.

That summer was the most defining time of my early adulthood. I did not care much for the job, which was mostly catering to rich doctors and lawyers living out a cowboy fantasy. Though I did make several friends, I tended to avoid the social cliques that formed among the ranch staff. Most of my free time was spent hiking and camping in the nearby mountains. Every summit reached was a moment where I felt as if muscular dystrophy had no impact on me. I was constantly pushing and chasing that feeling until it led me to the Camino four years later.

My Own Pace

As I climbed the hill to Cruz de Ferro, a rush of emotions flooded into my brain: relief to have reached this moment, fear for what lay ahead in my life, and joy for all I experienced on this journey. Suddenly, without any control, I began to cry. At many moments in my journey I shed tears when I encountered a difficult section and felt emotionally drained, but this was unlike any other time I cried in my adult life. My eyelids became swollen, and mucus filled my nose, causing me to cough as I sobbed. The only other time in my life I cried like this was the moment I learned the truth about a life with muscular dystrophy.

For most of my childhood, when I saw or heard of people being in wheelchairs with muscular dystrophy, I always assumed this did not apply to me. During all the childhood doctor visits, I was always told how good I was doing, how much I was growing, and how mild my case was. I was never told that in my adult years I would have more difficulties and might be in a wheelchair one day. I would probably live a near normal lifespan, but the average life expectancy is in the mid-forties. Just like any kid, I became stronger as I got older, so how was I to believe this would one day change? Surely my parents would have told me my condition was this serious.

When I was in seventh grade, I had a conversation with my sister about muscular dystrophy, and she mentioned me possibly needing a wheelchair later in life. My response was, "What do you mean?" The look on her face was a blank stare, as if she got caught accidentally revealing a surprise birthday party or spoiling the ending of a movie. My bottom lip began to quiver, and I asked, "Am I going to be able to walk my whole life?" In a shaky voice, she replied, "Probably not." Tears came flowing from my eyes, and I collapsed onto a couch. For twenty minutes, I cried and cried until my tear ducts were dry. My sister sat next to me, put her hand on my shoulder and silently comforted me. Deep inside I always knew what she told me, but this was the first time I heard it spoken. I needed to hear this, and my sister was probably the best person to tell me.

In one of her X chromosomes, she had the same genetic defect as me, inherited the same way, but being a female, her other X chromosome countered the defective one. In some sense, we shared the same disease, but I was the one who showed the symptoms. A 50/50 chance determined my condition. Sometimes as a teenager, I would sit in my room and flip a coin over and over, tails being muscular dystrophy and heads being no defect. Every time I got heads, I imagined never having this condition and when I got tails I was reminded the struggles were real. Other times I would wake up in the morning, lying still, hoping that when I got up my symptoms would be magically gone.

As I moved through high school, I began to resent my parents and doctors. I wondered if they knew of the knowledge I had about my future or if they would be mad at my sister for telling me. Occasionally, I researched online about my condition and cleared the browser history so my parents would not know what I was doing. Throughout my childhood, I witnessed my parents lie to people about where they were taking me when I went to doctors. On one family vacation we had our neighbors collect our mail, and my mom got upset when a Muscular Dystrophy Association newsletter was in the bundle returned to us. "Oh, I hope they don't know about this now," she said. Looking back, I understand that my parents were scared and did not know how to address the issue, but because of this, I began to feel ashamed of who I was. Whenever I sat out of gym class when running was involved, I always made an excuse to other students about hurting my knee or a simple, "I have a doctor's note" and not elaborating. Even close friends were kept in the dark about my condition.

There was a lot of anger in me during these years of my childhood where I felt mad at the world for giving me the life I had. I was secretly plagued by self-esteem issues, and during my middle school and early high school years, I teetered on the edge of becoming a troubled person. These were the years I grew long hair, listened to heavy metal music, wore a lot of black, and tried to create an identity where I saw myself as better than others in an effort to become disconnected from the parts of my life I could not change. I managed to keep my life on track, but the practice of hiding my muscular dystrophy stuck with me up until I came to the Camino. I felt that people would think less of me or treat me differently if they knew about my condition, but the kindness of others on the Camino taught me that it is better to be honest about who you are than to hide from something you cannot control. Finding the limits of my strength did not have to be about pretending my weakness did not exist, but about accepting the person I was.

As I thought about the anger I once felt regarding my diagnosis, my thoughts returned to the burden I was to leave behind at Cruz de Ferro. Clearly my burden was having muscular dystrophy, but how could I leave this behind? I then remembered what Logan said the day before about my rock representing anything I wanted. Maybe this was not about leaving something behind, but rather taking something with me, or swapping the rock for something else. This rock had been in my possession since my twentieth birthday when I took it from the top of Medicine Bow Peak. At that time, my accomplishment was subliminally rooted in denial, and now my understanding of strength had changed. What I sought on the Camino was to embark on an adventure while my body still allowed it, and that meant embracing truth. Muscular dystrophy would be a part of me for the rest of my life. People cannot always choose their burdens, but they can choose how they carry them. When I put my rock down, it would not be to let go of a burden, but to swap it for truth.

As I climbed the uneven pile of rocks, I slipped at the top and landed on my knees at the base of the wooden pole. I took one more look at my rock and placed it next to the pole.

Carrying My Burden

I recalled reading in the book by Viktor Frankl I had finished several days before, where he explained that every moment in life is a chance to change everything we were in the moment before. This moment at Cruz de Ferro, on September 17, was the moment I chose what my future would be. I let go of the past, embraced the present, and accepted my burden. Maybe a wheelchair was in my future, but I was headed there no matter what. The only other option was to continue down a dark path. I forgave my parents for keeping information from me throughout my childhood. Countless resources were always available to learn the truth, and nothing my parents could have said would have changed anything. There was no reason to resent anyone. Love is the only force in life worth believing in.

"Bryan!" I heard someone call out, and I looked up to see Father Cornelius heading toward me up the pile of rocks.

"Father Cornelius! Can you take my picture?" I asked, as I sat down at the top of the rocks. He took my camera and snapped a few pictures.

Walking down from the pile, I lost my balance, but Father Cornelius grabbed my pack and my left arm to keep me from falling. At the bottom, I looked back at the cross and started to cry again.

"Hey, you're alright," he said, as he gave me a hug and patted me on the shoulder.

"I never thought I would make it this far. I never thought I would ever be able to do something like this in my life," I said.

"With God anything is possible."

"I think you're right," I said, before I bid my final farewell to Father Cornelius.

"You are going to make it to Santiago. God is with you."

I had found God, but not in the Christian sense of the word. My God was in myself, in the moment, in the here and now. By definition I was probably still an agnostic, but humans are too special not to consider the possibility of a divine creation. The way Naomi explained God several weeks earlier made more sense, when she said, "There are more ways to believe in God than there are people on Earth, but you do not have to believe in God to believe in God." There is still a way to believe in God without dogmas and institutions because there is something greater that everyone can appreciate in the world. On the Camino, I came to appreciate faith. Regardless of someone's beliefs, we are all capable of love and compassion toward others. My own pace had been found in both a physical and spiritual sense.

As I continued on from Cruz de Ferro, I felt lighter, even though the rock I left behind had little weight. I felt more confident in the rest of my journey and the rest of my life. There are always unknown hardships looming ahead, but we need to embrace the life we have been given, and find our inner "grit." I knew I would make it to Santiago.

10

CALL ME "ROCKY"

While I was in El Acebo the evening after leaving my rock behind at Cruz de Ferro, a young blond-haired girl around twenty years old checked into the albergue I was staying at. Her eyes were full of tears as she dropped her pack to the ground and sat down on a bed next to mine. She stared blankly at her open palms that rested on her lap. I asked her if she was alright. She looked up and wiped the tears from her cheeks. She introduced herself as Sandra from Germany and told me about how hard the past few days had been since she began her Camino in León.

"Everything hurts," she said, with a look of defeat, and continued to say, "I do not think my body can go much farther."

"But if you've made it this far, you can do that distance again."

Sandra gestured to her head and her heart and said, "But everything is okay in here and in here."

"And that's all you need to finish a Camino," I said.

We talked for a few minutes, and I told her I had muscular dystrophy.

"How do you find such strength?" she asked.

"I just focus on my own pace. Just take one step at a time and eventually those steps will lead you somewhere," I said.

"You make it sound so easy," she said.

I laughed and said, "There is a saying in Finnish, jaksaa jaksaa, meaning to have enough strength to continue further. Sometimes I say that over and over in my head when I walk. If you believe you have that strength, you will find it."

"Where do you learn these things?"

"I met a lot of people on my Camino who taught me these things. They changed the way I look at the world," I said.

"Jaksaa, jaksaa," Sandra said, as her spirit seemed lifted.

Suddenly I remembered the promise I made to George to give the book *Man's Search for Meaning* to another pilgrim. Sandra seemed like a good candidate. I dug into my pack and pulled out the book.

"I don't know how much of a reader you are, but I have a book that might help you. Another pilgrim gave it to me, and I enjoyed it. Pass it along once you finish it."

After Sandra examined the front and back cover, she said, "Thanks. Looks interesting."

Suddenly, I realized giving a book about a Holocaust survivor to a German might have been in poor taste. Nevertheless, she seemed pleased by the book and continued saying, "I've been trying to spend less time on my phone, so this should help with that." I would never know if the book had a positive impact on Sandra, or if she even read it. I did not talk to her the rest of that evening, and I never saw her again.

Later that afternoon, I ran into Connor coming out of his room when I went to the bathroom down the hall. He and Evelyn had arrived shortly after me and were still settling in for the night. I asked Connor if they were having dinner at the albergue, and they said they were, so we agreed to all eat together.

After my rest, I went downstairs to sit on the front porch to watch the sunset over the mountains and wait for dinner. As I sat quietly watching the golden orange rays of light dip below a distant mountain, I heard Connor's voice from behind say, "It's beautiful isn't it?"

Turning around, I said, "Yeah, it's peaceful up here in the mountains."

"We still have to go through those mountains," Connor said.

"Yeah, I keep telling myself that I made it over the Pyrenees, so I can make it over these."

"Well, it's all worth it for these views," Connor said.

The trail would continue down into a valley for three days, before returning into the mountains, for a difficult climb to the town of O Cebreiro. From what I read and discussed with other pilgrims, hiking to O Cebreiro is considered the most difficult portion of the Camino. The steep incline and rocky trail requires scrambling in some locations and catches many off guard so close to Santiago.

"Sometimes beauty like this makes me sad," Connor said, with a serious expression as he squinted at the view.

"How do you figure?"

"Not everyone gets to appreciate views like this. There are people who never had the opportunity to explore the world. I think that's why I'm here now."

I knew he was thinking about his daughter, but still he chose not to share the story of her with me. He was quiet for several minutes, and I knew he was fighting the urge to tell me. After his silence, Connor talked about the upcoming obstacles, and then we went inside where Evelyn joined us. We all took a seat in the brightly lit dining room. Though I had seen Connor yesterday and today, this was the first time I saw Evelyn since Azofra. She had the same motherly look I remembered with her thick glasses and short curly grey hair.

The conversation at dinner focused on Camino food. Connor and Evelyn knew a lot about Spanish cuisine after hiking the Camino three other times. I was not looking forward to the increase in seafood as we neared the coast. Bocadillo jamón was keeping me alive. Connor told me his favorite Spanish food was chocolate con churros, and said he would treat me to some when we reached Santiago. Making plans for once I arrived in Santiago felt strange since it was always so far away, but now there were only one hundred fifty-six miles remaining. Those miles would be some of the most difficult. I felt particularly worried about tomorrow's incredibly steep and rocky section. After our dessert, which was only a few mouthfuls of ice cream, we all went to sleep.

I planned to stay at the same albergue as Connor and Evelyn the next night in the town of Ponferrada, so we knew we would see each other again there. Being with familiar pilgrims again felt good. I slept well that night and heard a minimal amount of snoring. The sound of steady rain on the roof was relaxing, but I knew it would make tomorrow's rocky section of trail slippery.

I was ready to leave the next morning at the usual time, until I saw that the road was dark with a dense, thick fog. Not wanting to be hit by a car, I waited for more light and was not walking until 7:30. This was the latest I started out since my first week on the Camino. Ponferrada was only nine miles away, so this would be one of my shortest days so far. The Camino followed the main road for about a mile, and then it became a dirt trail through a foggy mountain valley. Once the sun broke through the fog, the surrounding mountains were aglow in a reddish tint. Because of last night's rain, all of the trees were wet and emitted bright shades of green. The dirt road was flat and gravelly with a steady downward incline, allowing me to relax and enjoy the scenery.

Upon arriving in the village of Riego de Ambrós, I tried to find a café but nothing was open. The architecture was similar to El Acebo with brick buildings, wooden balconies, and dark slate roofs. Near the far edge of town, the Camino led off the road and onto a forested dirt trail. Several massive chestnut trees with long, thick twisting branches were clustered together, looking like something from a fairytale with eerie features warning me not to approach and to turn back.

Call Me "Rocky"

Beyond the trees began the most treacherous section of the trail I had encountered yet. Slick rock plunged downhill for several hundred feet. Almost immediately, I lost my balance, and my legs went up in the air like a cartoon character. I went down hard, hitting my tail bone on a sharp rock. A jolt of pain shot up my spine, and I yelled out in agony as I rolled over onto my stomach. I thought for sure my tail bone was broken. I wiggled off my pack and crawled to the side of the trail. To my relief, the pain eased up after a few minutes, but I would have yet another nasty bruise by morning. Back on my feet, I hoisted my pack over my shoulders and found my balance for a few more steps, but my confidence was shaken. A few feet farther, I slipped and fell again. This time my shoulder slammed into a grassy patch of ground. Again, I crawled to the side of the trail and waited for the pain to fade. I continued on, but taking no chances, I slid down the last portion of rock on my hands and sore rear as I kicked my pack ahead of me.

The trail leveled out into a section of flat dirt, but the relief was short-lived. Ahead was another few hundred feet of steep, smooth rock. Once again, I took off my pack and carefully crawled down the trail. A German pilgrim approached from behind. She looked at me on the ground and asked "Are you okay?"

"Yeah, I'm fine. I just took a fall, so I'm being careful," I said.

"I guess it's better to be safe than sorry," she laughed in a sarcastic tone.

I brushed off the awkwardness and continued on until the trail flattened out and followed the main road before moving back into the rocky terrain. There was another section of jagged rocks that required me to crawl and drag my pack again. I got a few more odd looks from a group of three young Korean pilgrims, dressed in bright red rain jackets, who were resting on the side of the trail. I assured them I was alright as I slowly crawled by. Making it over the rough section was a relief, and

157

My Own Pace

I took my time for the last stretch into the town of Molinaseca. I had only walked five miles from El Acebo, yet I was already completely beat up. Somewhere in the midst of my falls I got a long scrape on the bottom of my right forearm. With adrenaline pumping, it is easy to miss a minor injury. I was relieved to arrive in Ponferrada that evening, knowing there would be a break from mountains for the next two days.

On September 21, I finally began the climb into the mountains of Galicia. In the village of Herrerías, I overheard a few pilgrims talking about thunderstorms arriving later in the day. Most people were stopping here or in La Faba, midway up the climb, instead of risking a storm on top of O Cebreiro. A few dark clouds were moving in, but I figured I had enough time to make it to La Faba. Stopping in Herrerías would cost me an entire day, and my body was feeling strong. A man in Herrerías was handing out flyers offering horseback rides to O Cebreiro for a small fee. The horses left in an hour. I gave the offer some thought but opted to keep walking. If I skipped the most difficult section of the trail, I would never feel like I completed the Camino.

Almost immediately after Herrerías the trail became steeper, and I began moving at my slow pace. The humidity was rising, so I stopped to take a layer of clothing off and cool down. The hill had my heart pounding, and I made sure to slow down and to catch my breath. "Jaksaa, jaksaa," I repeated over and over to myself.

"Are you alright?" I heard a man with an American accent ask from behind. I turned to see a tall, broad shouldered man with a scruffy beard approaching.

"Yeah, I'm alright. I have muscular dystrophy," I said, as he began walking next to me and introduced himself as Carl from San Diego.

"Now, I don't know very much about the effects of MS but how does it affect you on the Camino?" Carl asked.

"No, I don't have MS, I have muscular dystrophy, MD.

Call Me "Rocky"

MS is multiple sclerosis. That's completely different," I said.

"I apologize for my ignorance," he said.

"Nah, it's alright. It's a common mistake. MD makes it hard walking up hills and over rough terrain."

"Does it get worse over time?" Carl asked.

"Yeah, it slowly gets worse over time as my muscle cells die. I will most likely be in a wheelchair later in my life," I said.

"You'll probably kill a lot of cells walking up this hill," Carl laughed.

"Well, it doesn't quite work like that," I said.

"Where did you start your Camino?" he asked quickly.

"St-Jean," I said.

"I'll be damned. Me too. No one says you're going to be in a wheelchair. You've made it this far. Look at me, I'm in my sixties, and I walked nearly four hundred miles. Only God knows what is possible," he said.

"Yeah, I just take it a day at a time. That's the only reason I made it this far," I said.

"A day at a time? I never plan to walk farther than the brim of my hat. There's not much farther ahead in life you can plan than that," Carl said.

"I like that. I always say if I can take one step then I can take another, and so on and so on," I said.

"You inspired me already. I'll see you later Bryan," he said, and moved ahead.

The trail became even steeper, moving off the paved road and onto a dirt trail that disappeared into the forest. With a mile and a half left to La Faba, the trail was littered with large rocks that consistently slowed me down.

"Just keep breathing. Just keep taking that next step," I said to myself.

The switchbacks up the mountain seemed to be endless, and around every turn I was disappointed to see more rocks and more uphill. These "false summits" as they are known, were extremely discouraging because I would put all my energy into what I thought was the last push to the top only to find that it still went higher. A few rocky sections were so steep that I had to take my pack off, lift it over a rock, and crawl up.

Along one difficult portion, a bald middle-aged Irish man with a young daughter around six years old with strawberry red hair approached as I hoisted my pack over another boulder. They asked if I was alright and continued walking. The girl turned around to watch as I struggled up the hill, and she asked, "What's wrong with your legs?"

Her father ushered the girl to keep walking, but she stayed to talk. I explained I had a muscle disease called muscular dystrophy. The father gave in once he saw I was not bothered to talk.

"What is that?" she asked.

"It means that my muscles are not as strong as yours and some things are harder for me."

"My legs hurt bad too," she said.

"I'm sure you're stronger than most people your age. Walking the Camino is tough."

The girl smiled and looked back at her father.

He gave a gentle smile and asked, "Where did you begin your Camino?"

I told him I started in St-Jean, and he explained that he and his daughter were walking from León to Santiago. Before they continued on, the daughter asked, "Can I give you something?"

I accepted, and she pulled a yellow flower out of her hair and handed it to me. I tucked it into one of the straps on my pack and thanked her.

"Mommy said we are supposed to give to others who are in need. She's in heaven now, but I will see her again after I'm an old lady."

"Oh, I'm sorry to hear that."

"It's okay. Daddy said Mommy is still with us, even when we walk on the Camino."

Call Me "Rocky"

"I'm sure she's proud of you."

The father, whose eyes began to look watery and glazed, ushered his daughter to continue.

"My name is Rose. What's your name?"

"I'm Bryan. It was nice to meet you Rose," I said, as she reached out her tiny hand to give me a firm handshake.

"Buen Camino, Bryan," she said.

I began thinking about Rose's mother and wondered how someone so young was able to understand the concept of death. Rose took solace in the idea that she would see her mother again one day. Perhaps someone her age could not process a person going away and never coming back. Death had been on my mind the year leading up to my Camino. I had many people close to me pass away, including my last three grandparents. My two grandmothers died, one from cancer and the other from complications from a broken hip, and my grandfather passed away from Alzheimer's the week before I began my Camino. As he was in his final weeks of life and my trip was planned, the possibility existed of his death coinciding with my journey. I wondered if I would have to cancel or postpone my trip. He would have wanted me to continue with my plans no matter what. Things worked out, but I wondered what my grandparents would have thought about my journey. My grandmothers would have been worried wrecks, but I knew they would have been proud of me. Because of this, they were with me on this journey in a spiritual sense. Sometimes when I saw an older pilgrim I would think of them. Other times when the trail was tough, my memory of them provided an extra bit of encouragement. After my conversation with Rose, I felt their presence a little more than usual.

As I continued climbing up the mountain I kept saying, "jaksaa, jaksaa" in my head. As soon as you think you do not have the ability to reach your goal, you will never make it there. You must believe in yourself to keep going. I wished Ella, Beth, Alma, Regina, or anyone else from my first days on the Camino could be with me now as I struggled up the mountain. They would have lent a hand or said some encouraging words, but it was time to face this mountain alone. My burdens were mine. Everyone I met along the journey played their role and gave me the wisdom to believe I had the strength to continue. Even if they were not physically here now, they were still with me.

"Jaksaa, jaksaa."

As I sat down on a large rock to catch my breath an older German woman passed and asked if I was alright.

"Yeah, just catching my breath," I said.

"They call it a stairway to heaven because it isn't easy getting there," she said, as she passed by.

Feeling inspired by the woman's words, I swung my pack back on my shoulders and continued on to La Faba. My muscles were sore and stiff as I inched up the steep trail and just when I thought La Faba would never arrive, I saw a distant building, and knew I was close. The town was small with steep and narrow cement streets. Several stone walls, covered in lichen and thick clumps of grass, bordered most of the streets. The stone buildings with large wooden doors were covered in ivy and had clusters of trees around them. I found an albergue at the far end of town where I decided to spend the night. The heavy rain storm finally rolled through in the late afternoon, and I knew I made the right choice to save reaching O Cebreiro until tomorrow.

The temperature during the night dropped below thirty degrees. Higher elevations were always colder, and I would still be heading higher yet. I knew the trail would be rocky and difficult to navigate in the dark, and I wasn't prepared for below freezing temperatures, so I waited until after sunrise to begin walking.

The trail from La Faba to the village of Laguna de Castilla was a little over a mile but it was rocky and rough. I stumbled over several loose rocks but managed to keep from falling.

162

Call Me "Rocky"

After passing through the woods, I emerged above the tree line and saw a colorful sunrise with a thick layer of clouds trapped in the mountain valley. Known as a cloud inversion, this rare occurrence caused a billowy white layer to flow between the mountains like a river, even splitting around a peak. Hidden beneath the clouds was La Faba. Gazing at the view of mountains in every direction made this location feel remote and desolate. Several pilgrims were gathered here photographing the scenery.

Midway between La Faba and Laguna was a steep section with a lot of slick, flat rock, and huge boulders that required some scrambling to get over. I was about to take my pack off, throw it over the rocks and climb, when two French pilgrims approached from behind. One was short with thick black hair, while the other was tall and skinny with short grey hair and a goatee. The skinny man said something in French and gestured toward the obstacle as if to ask, "Do you need help?"

I handed him my backpack, and he carried it over the boulders as I crawled up. The other man offered me his hand over one of the rocks and helped pull me up as my feet slid and struggled to get a firm grip. I expected him to return my pack, but he slung it over his shoulder with his own pack and walked slowly as we continued up. He carried my pack for several hundred feet until the trail leveled out, and he handed it back to me.

"Thank you so much," I said, and shook his hand. He and his companion smiled and nodded, understanding my gratitude, despite the language barrier.

Within a few minutes another steep, rocky section appeared. At the top I saw the two same pilgrims waiting. How could they be so kind? Their first thought when they saw the difficult section was to wait for me because they knew I would need help. The man, who carried my pack before, walked back down the steep section, grabbed my pack again and carried it up the hill as I climbed.

My Own Pace

"No words can express how grateful I am for your help," I said, as he handed back my pack at the top of the hill.

Again he simply smiled and nodded his head as he continued on ahead. That was the last I saw those two men. Like all the other pilgrims I met on the Camino, their story crossed paths with mine for a brief moment before we continued at our own paces. The village of Laguna came into view, and I continued up a slow incline into the settlement. There were only a few homes here, along with several stone barns with rusty metal doors. Tractors and scattered pieces of farm equipment were alongside the road. I passed a lone café, but decided not to stop because I did not know how long it would take to reach O Cebreiro. I wanted to save all my resting for the end of the day. If I could survive the next two miles, the most difficult parts of the Camino would be behind me. My spirits were higher than ever on my thirty-sixth day. Somehow I walked the majority of the Camino with little more than a few scratches and bruises. In just over a week I planned to be in Santiago. I estimated that I needed between nine or ten more days.

The last mile into O Cebreiro became flatter and went through a thick grove of trees with long twisted branches, eventually leading onto a paved road into town. The view here was magnificent. Mountains rose up from the sides of a deep green valley dotted with farms and small homes cut into the hills. The distant rooftops of La Faba were visible under a backdrop of mountains, and the sun was aligned perfectly with the valley, ruining any chance of a good picture, but perfectly illuminating my entry to O Cebreiro. The mountains of the Camino no longer scared me. My only fear now was if the insights I gained would resonate throughout my life.

As I continued through the town, the small size shocked me since my guidebook said the town had a population of over one thousand. This seemed like a mistake since I only saw about fifteen tightly packed buildings, most of which were cafés and albergues. I expected more out of the town that was famously rumored to be where the Holy Grail was hidden. I was out of the village as quickly as I arrived. There was one last major hill to climb after O Cebreiro, which was the actual 4,300 foot summit before the hike down from the mountains. I walked slowly up the steep hill, and the view from the top was of another deep valley mostly hidden in clouds. The land before me was lush with vibrant shades of green resembling a fairytale land. This was Galicia!

The next day as I continued down the mountain, after spending the night in a small village called Hospital, an American couple from California named Donnie and Noelle began to walk with me as my slow pace blocked their path. Donnie was tall with red hair, and long skinny legs that looked furry with the same color hair as his head. Noelle was short, with long jet-black hair, wearing yoga pants, and brown hiking shoes on her tiny feet that gracefully navigated the rocks. They asked if I was alright when I was going slow and relying heavily on my hiking pole.

"It sure is a rocky road," Donnie said.

"Rocky Raccoon Road," Noelle laughed, as she started singing "Rocky Raccoon" by The Beatles.

"Oh God, I'm going to have that song stuck in my head all day now," I said, as Noelle sang the song in a slow soothing voice.

They moved ahead, but I ran into them again coming out of a café in the town of Biduedo.

"I don't remember your name, but I'm going to call you Rocky Raccoon," Noelle said.

"It's Bryan!" I said.

"No, it's Rocky Racoon!"

"Do you have a trail name yet?" Donnie asked.

"No, I thought trail names were an American thing, not a Camino thing," I said.

"Well, you're an American aren't you?"

"Yes," I laughed. "Do you guys have trail names?"

"I'm Medusa, and this is Beavertail," Noelle said, as she pointed to Donnie.

"And my name is Rocky Raccoon," I laughed.

When I arrived in the town of Triacastela where I was spending the night, I passed a crowded café down the road, and I heard a girl call out, "Rocky!"

I turned and saw Medusa and Beavertail eating under an awning of an outside café. I figured this was a good place to have lunch, so I sat down with them and ordered a bocadillo jamón.

"What day did you start in St-Jean?" Beavertail asked, as I got comfortable in a seat.

"August 18," I said.

"Really? We started on August 25. Have you been taking a lot of rest days? Or did you get injured?" Medusa asked.

"I only took a few rest days. But I have muscular dystrophy, so I've been going at a slower pace," I said.

"Well, I'm impressed. You've got to be stronger than anyone we've met to make it this far, with what you've probably had to go through. We should call you Rocky Balboa, not Rocky Raccoon," Medusa said.

I chatted with them as I finished my sandwich and continued on to find an albergue in town. They were continuing on to the next village of A Balsa so I did not know if I would see them again.

"Your trail name found you for a reason. Someone named Rocky doesn't give up. They fight until the end. We'll see you in Santiago," Beavertail exclaimed as I walked away.

The next day after I left the town of Sarria, I passed the marker showing one hundred kilometers (sixty-two miles) to Santiago. Pilgrims only needed to hike the last hundred kilometers to be awarded the certificate at the end, so the most crowded section of trail began in Sarria. The cement block was covered with signatures, words of wisdom, stones placed on top, and notes tucked into the pile of rocks. Blue paint around the yellow arrow made it appear to glow. This should have been a joyous moment, but I was in pain I could ignore no longer. My right hip and the tendons behind my knees were hurting, and I felt like I was falling apart.

Dark thoughts filled my mind like they had the day I arrived in St-Jean. I thought for sure I was done, and this hip pain would end my journey. If my knee or hip became more inflamed, there was no way I could finish the remaining sixty-two miles. I remembered Florence saying that the Camino was not worth an injury she would regret for the rest of her life. Maybe I would be forced to make the same decision. Why did I walk all the way from St-Jean? Maybe I should have just started in Sarria like everyone else. Was I really on the Camino just to receive a certificate that verified I completed the walk, nothing more than a silly piece of paper? I tried to recall the feelings I had at Cruz de Ferro where I felt I had all the answers. If I had already grown on this journey and accepted muscular dystrophy, why did I need to walk farther?

Shortly after the one hundred kilometer marker, an American couple passed me as they prayed the Rosary out loud. When I heard them praying, I started to cry. My body was telling me it had had enough of the Camino. All the people I knew who ended their journeys lost faith before me, and now it was my turn. As my eyes became watery, I began saying out loud the Lord's Prayer I heard the American couple repeating. Maybe I was not truly a Catholic, but hopefully this would help.

After I finished wiping a few stray tears from my eyes, a group of about thirty pilgrims, who had obviously started their Camino in Sarria, passed by. Seeing my large pack, which none of them had, a tall British man in the group asked where I began my Camino. I said I started in St-Jean, and the entire group stopped and turned to look at me. Apparently I was the first pilgrim they met who started in St-Jean. Several of the pilgrims came over and shook my hand and patted me on the shoulder.

"Can we take a picture with you?" a couple in the group asked.

"I guess so," I said softy, and they handed their camera to someone in the group, and five pilgrims all gathered around me for a picture.

The situation had me perplexed, and it felt weird to be the subject of such happiness and joy when I was just crying over the thought that I would never make it to Santiago. Everyone in the group said, "Buen Camino" as they passed, and my mood began to improve. I realized that being an inspiration to others can sometimes be a source of great strength. I had walked from St-Jean, and I had the ability to finish the Camino. Father Cornelius's voice suddenly came into my thoughts, "You are going to make it to Santiago. God is with you."

Despite my optimism, the next morning in the town of Portomarín, I awoke in more pain than the day before. My legs were still stiff, and I had a clicking sensation in my right hip along with a sharp pain. I left at the usual time of 5:30, thinking that walking would warm me up and the pain would subside. My planned destination for the day was nearly eleven miles away in the town of Ligonde. After coming out of Portomarín and crossing a small bridge over a dry stream bed, I began limping and shifting my weight onto my good hip, but the pain still increased. Every step was a battle not only against pain, but against my body physically refusing to move. I made it to the main road, about a mile and a half outside of Portomarín, but I would never make the distance to Ligonde.

Continuing farther with a hurt hip could cause damage that might prevent me from walking the last fifty miles. All I had to do was be in Santiago by October 6, so I could catch my flight on October 7. Today's date was September 26, which meant this was my fortieth day on the trail. At ten miles a day, I would be in Santiago on October 1. There was still a lot of time, but pushing my body too hard could easily give me an injury that would put me several days behind schedule. I wished I remained in Portomarín for a rest day, but all I could do now was stay in the nearest town up the road. My guidebook listed the nearby village of Castromaior, so I hoped to find accommodations there.

As the dirt trail continued along the side of the road, it entered a dense wooded section with a thick canopy. From behind I heard a man's voice call out, "Hey, Rocky!" I turned to see Beavertail and Medusa.

"Hey, how are you guys?" I asked.

"We're fine, but how are you?" Medusa asked, looking at my legs.

"I have hip pain. It's bad," I said.

"Do you have any pain medication?" Beavertail asked.

"Nah, I don't have anything," I said.

"You're walking the Camino without pain medication? You truly are Rocky Balboa."

"Yeah, well . . ." I began to say when the husband interjected. "Here take this."

He dug into a side pocket of his pack and handed me four packaged ibuprofen tablets. "Take one now and save the others for later. They are six hundred milligrams, so one should do it," he said.

"Wow, thanks. Yeah, this should help. I'm going to stop early today so I can rest," I said.

"No problem. Good luck," he said, as they disappeared ahead, and I never saw them again.

The Camino never failed to provide.

11
FINAL STEPS

The pain medication the American couple gave me kicked in just as I arrived in Castromaior. Though I was disappointed to stop early, the change in plans caused me to run into two familiar faces the next morning. Connor and Evelyn! We began to walk together down a shaded road, and I realized that despite knowing them since my first week on the trail, this was my first time actually walking with them. I found their similar slow pace to be relaxing.

Not long after I began walking with them, a car approached us from behind, and as we moved to the side of the road, I tripped and fell. Connor helped me to my feet, and I brushed off the fall until I realized my hiking pole had broken. The metal shaft was completely bent, making it unbalanced and almost useless.

"I don't know what I will do now," I said with a heavy sigh.

"Connor, give him one of our poles. We don't need two anymore," Evelyn said.

"No, I can't accept that from you. You might need it."

"Don't be silly. You need it more than we do," Connor insisted.

"Are you sure?" I asked.

"Of course," Connor replied, as he handed me one of his green-colored poles.

Final Steps

I leaned my broken pole against a cement trail marker. Leaving it behind was a bit emotional, so I snapped a picture. This pole helped me over four hundred fifty miles, across the Pyrenees, through the Meseta, and into Galicia. I had planned to mail it home before my flight, but Connor's pole now had more sentimental value. I could think of no better memento from this journey. This pole was given to me when I was in need, allowing the kindness of others to remain with me.

As we walked, our conversations turned deeper, and Evelyn abruptly asked, "Do you ever wish you were never born with muscular dystrophy?"

This question caught me off guard, and I hesitated for a moment. I realized I had never been asked that before. My immediate thought was to say yes, since having a degenerative muscle disease has no inherent benefit, but maybe the answer was not so simple. When I sat out of gym class in school and watched other kids run and have fun, I would always tell myself, "I wish I never had muscular dystrophy." These complicated thoughts continued up until I came to the Camino, but it was in these dark contemplations that I ultimately came to terms with my uncertain future and changed the way I viewed my burden. My experience living with muscular dystrophy made me who I was, and I was happy with the person I had become.

"No I don't wish that," I finally answered to Evelyn.

"Oh," Evelyn said quietly, as she registered my response.

"We all have just one chance to live our lives, so feeling sorry for ourselves and wishing for a different life won't get us anywhere. Life isn't meant to be easy. We have to embrace the life we have and enjoy it for what it is," I said.

"But what does this life mean? What is the purpose of all this suffering we go through in life, all of the disease, death, and hardship?" Evelyn asked.

"Well, that's the age old question, isn't it," I said, as I pondered an answer, then I continued to say, "Maybe it doesn't

171

mean anything. Maybe that's what makes our lives so special. I think sometimes that is more comforting of a thought than to believe we are special as humans. We are all just little specks in this world, and our world and our galaxy are even smaller specks in the universe, and beyond that, who knows how insignificant our universe really is."

My answers continued to surprise Evelyn, and she did not seem to understand what I had to say. People spend their whole lives looking for reasons for all of our suffering, telling us what to do and which direction to go, but after walking nearly five hundred miles across Spain, I realized that we really do not know much at all. The only thing we really know is that we are alive, and the more I pushed my body to its limit, the more I was aware of that simple fact. Humans are capable of much more than we realize, on our own or with the help of others.

We arrived in Palas de Rei, the town where I planned to spend the night, around 10:30 a.m. I found the town to be much larger than expected with a population around four thousand. A major road through the center of town was lined with parked cars. After we came down a flight of cement steps between two streets, I found Albergue Castro where I made my reservation. The four-story building was on a tightly packed block of apartments, cafés, and dirty buildings that trapped the smell of car exhaust. Connor and Evelyn were continuing on to the village of O Coto, so we parted ways knowing that we would not see each other again until Santiago. I promised to send them an email when I arrived, and we would arrange a reunion.

The next morning on the trail, I was passed by a young woman with curly, unkempt brunette hair and an elderly bald man with a grey beard. I noticed he was limping and using two hiking poles. One of his poles was red with the lower shaft slightly bent. Suddenly I realized that was my old pole.

"Hey, where did you find that pole?" I asked.

Final Steps

The man looked at me with a blank stare as if he had no understanding of English. The woman, with a French accent and mannerisms suggesting an intellectual disability said, "He found it on the trail and fixed it. He was injured and needed another pole."

"Oh, that's great! I'm the one who left that pole there. I got a new one," I said, pointing to my hiking pole.

The young woman translated to the man, and he handed the pole back to me.

"No, it's yours now. I have a new one," I said, gesturing to my pole again, as he gave me a pat on my shoulder.

"I'm glad it found a good home," I said, and the woman translated to the old man.

"Je vous remercie," the man said, as they moved on ahead.

I was having some foot pain that morning despite taking some pain medication, but being able to help the man raised my spirits and took my mind off of the pain. There were few times I was able to offer significant help to someone, so this incident felt like an opportunity to give back to the Camino. So many occurrences on the Camino appeared to be interconnected. I could not help but think that I was meant to break my pole so that man could find it and make use of it. Just maybe, there are forces at play that humans cannot understand.

The next morning, after spending the night in the town of Melide, I was on the trail by 4:45. I found myself waking up earlier as I neared Santiago, and my excitement was building. Just over thirty miles remained. At this pace, I was looking at three more days on the trail. Today I would walk nine miles to Arzúa. The sun was not rising until after 8:00 a.m. now, so a large portion of my walk would be in darkness. Beyond Melide, the trail went through a dark forest of eucalyptus trees so dense that it was difficult to see my hand in front of my face without a headlamp.

As I made my way through the woods, up ahead I saw the

flicker of a candle burning on the side of the trail. This was a stamp station where pilgrims could stamp their credentials on the small table decorated with several shells and rocks. In the darkness beyond a cluster of trees, I heard a menacing growl. After looking around, my headlamp focused on a pair of glowing eyes and what looked like the silhouette of a wolf. I knew there were wolves in Galicia, but I did not expect to see one.

After concluding in my mind that there was a hungry wolf about to maul me, I left as quickly as I could, only to be stopped several feet away at a wide stream with a crude rock bridge stretching to the other side. With my unsteady legs, I knew it was too dark to attempt a crossing without help, so I stood there in an almost frozen state. I could still hear the growling. Now I was trapped between the wolf and the river. I felt like I was in a nightmare as the candle flickered strange shadows throughout the trees. My dim headlamp did little to penetrate the darkness. I heard sticks snapping all around me, and thought I was being surrounded by a pack of wolves.

After several moments of eternity, the growling turned to grunting, and then to loud sniffling. I realized I was hearing the sound of snoring. Feeling confused, I looked at the stamp station again and saw it had "Donkey Stamp" written on the stand in red paint. I realized the wolf was actually a donkey. The man who ran the station was asleep and camped out with his donkey. An enormous feeling of relief and humiliation rushed over me. I should have immediately recognized the sound of snoring after all I heard in the albergues.

The rock bridge did not seem so difficult now, so I decided to conquer it without daylight or the help of others. With high spirits and wobbly legs, I carefully made my way across the bridge, which at some places appeared narrower than my foot in the darkness. I nearly lost my balance but caught myself with my hiking pole. After facing the "donkey wolf" and the bridge, I felt invincible and relaxed about the rest of the day. Onward to Santiago!

Final Steps

On October 2, my forty-sixth day on the trail, I woke up at 3:45 a.m. and started walking. I had spent the night in the village of Monte de Gozo, which was just three miles short of Santiago. I wanted to make sure I had a short walk on the day I arrived in Santiago so I could be at the Cathedral before the crowds of tourists. The road was all downhill as I made my way into the outskirts of Santiago. As I walked through the cobblestone streets, I felt as if my feet were carrying me without any thought, but I was extra careful not to fall during these last few miles. That would be just my luck to walk five hundred miles and get injured at the very end.

I lost track of the yellow arrows in the city and asked for directions to find the Cathedral. When I finally rounded the corner to the Cathedral Square, it was completely empty. I followed the path to the official end point, dropped my pack to the ground, raised my fists in the air like the statue of Rocky in Philadelphia, and then collapsed to my knees looking up at the Cathedral with teary eyes. The Cathedral was under renovation and sections of it were covered with blue tarps and scaffolding, but three large pointed spires topped with crosses were still visible. The sight was breathtaking, but seeing the Cathedral was not the reason I walked five hundred miles to Santiago. The journey was the destination.

I took a deep breath and lay back on the ground. The dark sky was slowly giving way to twilight as the last few stars still twinkled. The mornings were always one of my favorite parts of the Camino, when the entire day was ahead of me, and who I might meet and where I would spend the night was unknown. This morning was different because I was already where I needed to be. I closed my eyes and felt a cool breeze against my face. This journey began in the intense summer heat of August, and now it was fall. My meditation was abruptly disturbed as the roar of a street cleaning car came from around the bend of a side street. I quickly got to my feet as the vehicle headed in my direction. Several people were now walking around the square, and the city was waking up. I was glad to have those few minutes alone.

On a bench in the Cathedral Square, I had a breakfast of granola bars, and called home to let my family and several friends know I had finished the Camino de Santiago. After eating, I walked down an old cobblestone road to the pilgrim office around 7:45 to receive my Compostela. There were already many pilgrims outside the unassuming white building waiting for the office to open at 8:00. The line moved slowly, but I was early enough to beat the main crowd.

As the line of pilgrims wound through a brightly lit hallway, awaiting judgment from one of the many clerks at a long wooden counter, a mix of emotions ran through my brain. I had just completed the greatest challenge of my life, yet I was just another pilgrim among hundreds of others. There was no music playing, no cheering crowds, no balloons, or people waiting for me at the end. There was nothing special about anyone. We were all the same.

I made it to the counter, and I showed the woman my credential. She asked how my journey was and copied my information onto a sheet of paper. Anxiety kicked in, and I feared something would be wrong. Maybe I did not collect enough stamps or maybe she would not believe I walked the entire distance. I tried to keep my voice calm and slow and only relaxed once she pulled out a Compostela and wrote my name on it in Latin as Brennum Steward, certifying I had walked seven hundred ninety-nine kilometers from St-Jean-Pied-de-Port to Santiago de Compostela. The document had an intricate colorful border with a picture of Saint James in the upper right corner.

Just like that, I was done. I walked up a steep road to the albergue I would be staying at until my flight home in six days. The time was only 10:00, and it did not open until noon, so I got comfortable on a cement wall and watched the city come to life as hundreds of pilgrims found their way into the

Cathedral Square. Their expressions told hundreds of stories from beaming smiles to eyes full of tears. This was the place everyone dreamed of seeing since taking their first steps on the trail, and now this was the end of so many Camino stories. Whether someone is happy to be done or sad to leave this place behind, integrating the lessons of this journey into real life would become the next adventure. Shortly after I sat down, I heard a voice call out, "Hey, look who it is!"

I turned to find Connor and Evelyn coming toward me with big smiles. I jumped up and gave them big hugs, and they congratulated me on finishing the Camino.

"You did it!" Connor exclaimed.

"Only because you gave me your hiking pole," I said.

"Well, I don't want to take all the credit," Connor said.

After sitting for a few minutes, recounting the past few days, Connor said, "I would like to treat you to Santiago's famous chocolate con churros."

We walked through the city to the restaurant that Connor and Evelyn went to every time they were in Santiago. The large restaurant with a high ceiling and black marble floors felt too fancy for my dirty clothes, unkempt hair, large pack, and hiking pole. Once I sat down with other pilgrims scattered about in black leather chairs, I felt at home. The chocolate con churros were served on a white plate with gold edging and a mug of hot chocolate for dipping the churros in, and they tasted delicious. I was still numb to the feeling of just finishing the Camino and did not have a whole lot to say as we ate. After our snack, we took pictures of each other around the Cathedral. We agreed to meet the next evening for dinner before they flew home to Florida.

I made my way back to the albergue to check in. While I lay in bed, I sent a message to Ella to let her know I arrived in Santiago. I had last seen her when we parted ways in the village of Lorca many weeks ago. In a message she sent me a few days ago, she explained how she would still be in

Santiago when I arrived. We agreed to meet at 5:00 for a drink at a bar next to my albergue. She had to leave at 6:30 to catch her flight home to Finland with her mother. I took a shower, brushed my teeth, shaved, and made sure I looked the best I could after walking five hundred miles.

When I was outside the bar waiting for Ella, I heard a familiar Australian voice from the crowd behind me say, "Mr. America, you have done a truly magnificent thing."

I turned to find Ethan standing next to me. I reached out to shake his hand, and he gave me a hug.

"Did you finish today?" I asked.

"No, I finished yesterday but received my Compostela this morning," he said.

We talked for a few minutes about our plans for the coming days, and he said he was catching a flight back to Australia tomorrow. As we were talking, out of the corner of my eye I saw Ella making her way down the street toward me.

"Ella!" I yelled out, and she hurried over.

"Bryan!" she yelled, as we hugged and she said, "It's so good to see you."

"How are you?" I said.

"I'm great, but how are you? You made it!"

"I'm feeling great. I'm still in a little bit of shock that I'm actually here in Santiago," I said.

"I'm so happy for you!"

"Oh, and this is Ethan, we started the Camino on the same day," I said, as I introduced him.

Ethan had not met Ella on the Camino even though I met both of them during my first week. So many people I met were only days or moments away from never knowing me, but I found that the Camino brings everyone to you for a reason.

"I'll leave you guys to catch up," Ethan said, as he began to leave.

"Would you like to have a drink with us? We're going right here," I said, as I pointed to the bar.

Final Steps

"No, thank you. I need to run some errands here in the city. I'm sure I'll see you again today," he said.

We sat at an outside table, drank beer, and talked about everything that had happened since we parted ways. I told her all about my sickness, the bed bugs, all of my struggles over the mountains in Galicia, and my encounter with the donkey wolf.

Ella was able to work out the problems she was having with her mother and begin to heal their troubled relationship and end the resentment her mother felt for her leaving the United States to live in Finland. Her mother no longer introduced Ella as being American and accepted the life she chose to make for herself.

"So, what now?" I said, after a few moments of silence. "How do we go back to our other lives after the Camino?'

"It is a difficult thing going back to the complexities of life after being in such a simple place for so long," Ella said.

"Strange how our nomadic life has been so simple, but our stationary life seems so complicated," I said.

Ella laughed and said, "I'm really at the edge of so much uncertainty. I need to find an apartment when I get back to Helsinki and sign my contract for a year of work. That's as far as I have planned. I don't even know if I will be a nurse forever or even live in Finland forever."

"I'm in such an unknown part of my life too. I need to return to my part-time job that's going nowhere and continue to search for a full-time job. It almost makes me want to just screw the system, quit my job, and keep traveling," I said.

"What's stopping you?" Ella asked.

"Society," I laughed.

"But what's society got to do with it?" she asked.

"I don't know. I need a job. I need to start planning for the future," I said.

"But your job doesn't control you, you control you. No one is forcing you to do anything. We create most of the

179

chains that tie us down and prevent us from doing the things we love," Ella said.

"Yeah, I wish I could just keep hiking the Camino forever. Maybe my next adventure isn't far away," I said.

"The adventure doesn't have to end. You will find a way to do it. You figured out how to walk five hundred miles; you're capable of much more than you realize," Ella said.

"You're right. If you put your mind to anything, you can do it. I've definitely learned that on the Camino."

"People travel and work. There are a lot of hostels that will pay you to work for a season, and then you can travel with the money you make," Ella said.

"Yeah, it's something I can always consider," I said.

"Have you ever thought about volunteering at an albergue?"

"Yeah, I have, actually. It would be a good way to give back to the Camino," I said.

"It would be something fun to do with a group one day. It could be another way to experience the Camino. Perhaps we could do that one day," she said.

"Maybe we could. I feel like the Camino will find a way to come back into my life."

We continued talking about what we would do after we returned home and what we would miss the most about the Camino. As we were talking, Ethan spotted us and came over to say one last goodbye before he went back to his albergue for the evening. Ethan explained that he had met Angie for dinner the evening before in the city, and how Hazel finished the Camino the week before and continued traveling through Europe. I told Ethan about Beth and Alma, and how Alma was injured and Beth biked a large portion of the rest of the Camino, finishing the week before us. Seeing Ethan in Santiago seemed fitting. No one else on the Camino saw me on both the first and last day.

After Ethan left, I walked with Ella down the road as she

was going to meet with her group. My hip was hurting again, so I did not walk with her the rest of the way through the city.

"Will I see you again?" Ella asked, with a look of sadness in her eyes.

"I know we'll see each other again one day," I said.

"Jaksaa, jaksaa."

"Jaksaa, jaksaa," I repeated back as we hugged.

I stood in the middle of the bustling crowd and watched Ella walk toward the Cathedral, thinking about how sad I was when we parted ways in Lorca. This time I did not feel so sad. My fear was that I would never see her again on the Camino, but I did, just as we promised each other. Now my Camino was over, and it was time to return home.

12
JOURNEY'S END

On an afternoon in early February 2018, I sat on the snowy bank of the Delaware River watching small ice chunks float downstream. After a series of unusually frigid days across New Jersey, the weather was finally warm enough for a walk. A week earlier I quit my new job as a 9-1-1 dispatcher. What was I thinking taking a job as a dispatcher? This was something I should have known I could not handle. I was desperate to find full-time work and leave my part-time job at a local community college, so I accepted the first offer I received. Now I had no job and no direction. I felt like an utter failure as I stared across the river into Pennsylvania.

Bare tree branches swayed in the chilly wind as I listened to the roar of the river. I thought back to the warmer climate in Spain four months earlier. After returning home, I felt I was on the verge of a major breakthrough in my life, but now I felt defeated. Transitioning back to normal life after the Camino took more effort than I anticipated. Returning to work the morning after flying home was similar to running at full speed and hitting a brick wall. There were other difficult readjustments to normal life such as driving a car after not driving for two months and my sleep patterns being completely out of sync. After sleeping in a different place every night for nearly fifty days, I would wake up in a panic, jump out of bed and have no idea where I was as I searched for my backpack.

Journey's End

Once the panic subsided, I would realize I was home and not in an albergue. Luckily, this did not last more than a couple of weeks as my mind and body readjusted.

The hardest part of my return was surprisingly the attention I received. I wanted to return to normality, but no one was allowing me. My boss brought in a cake for my first day back to work, and everyone made a huge fuss that made me feel a little uncomfortable. Though I was grateful for their kindness and appreciation, I was simply overwhelmed. The challenge of explaining the trip to coworkers, friends, and family proved a daunting task. When someone said, "Tell me about your trip," I had no words to describe the experience. Most of the stories everyone wanted to hear were about food poisoning, bed bugs, and everything that nearly ruined my journey. I realized that the Camino cannot be told with pictures and stories; it must be experienced to be understood.

The college where I worked asked me to give a lecture about the Camino, and an article about my trip appeared on the college's website. I was also interviewed by a writer for my hometown newspaper, and the article was published in November. A simple walk down the street led to neighbors stopping and asking about my trip, and I received Facebook messages from old friends I had not talked to in years. For a while, the attention really bothered me, and I began to feel like the opposite of a person returning from a spiritual journey. I felt as if all the wisdom I gained was a lie. All of this hurt even more when people told me I was a hero to them, and I did not feel that way about myself. The real heroes were the ones who slowed down to help me and provided the wisdom that kept me motivated.

Slowly, I began to come around and emerge from my month-long funk, realizing that hiding away from the world solves nothing. While giving my lecture at the college, I recognized that the experiences and insights gained on the Camino were true, and I really had grown as a person. The lessons we learn do not always come instantaneously, but they appear once we allow them to. Despite this realization, now that I was unemployed, all I wanted to do was return to Europe and keep traveling. Maybe a part of me did not want to hold down a job and live a contemporary life. The Camino was one of the few places where everything made sense, and my life had the purpose I was seeking. Was this a dream I wanted to chase? Where would I find a job where I could take off several months and travel again? Was I bold enough to leave everything behind and hit the road full-time?

Surprisingly, the answer would come later that day after returning home from my walk along the river. While doing my usual scouring of the Internet for job postings, a position caught my attention. A local school that I attended as a child was hiring a teaching assistant with the primary function of school security. Initially I was hesitant to apply for a job related to teaching since I had no experience with children. The job was only part-time, and the pay was not great, but I would have summers off for traveling. Today was the last day applications were being accepted, so I applied. The following day I received a phone call from the school and was scheduled for an interview the next day.

When I arrived for the interview, both secretaries in the office immediately remembered me from when I was a student and from the newspaper article about my Camino. The story about my journey followed me everywhere. The interview with the principal was brief and ended with him saying, "You seem like a good guy, and the secretaries here seem to know you already. How soon can you start?" I interviewed on a Friday and started work on Monday.

The first day of work was surreal. All of my childhood teachers still worked at the school, which made returning there feel like a trip back in time. The job was not difficult as I did little more than sit by the front door to check-in visitors and late students, assist the dean during lunches, and substitute in

Journey's End

classrooms as needed. Working with children was something I swore I would never do, yet here I was. After working several odd jobs after graduating from college, I was finally doing something I enjoyed. The only problem was this job was not full-time. I was promised that the school district intended for the position to become full-time for the upcoming school year. I hoped this was true, but my only concern was having a job to come back to in September after having ten weeks off.

As the school year came to a close, I began making plans for a return to Europe. I was going back to the Camino, but this time I was going to hike the Portuguese Way, from Porto to Santiago, and then hike to Finisterre and some additional trails around Galicia. Reaching Finisterre would be the most important goal of the trip. The year before I felt slightly unfilled by not walking to the coast after Santiago, but now I would be able to reach the absolute end and have a completely new journey leading into it. The adventure was about to continue.

After a series of connecting flights, I arrived in Porto, Portugal late in the morning on July 8. I was immediately confused when I landed and had no idea how to find my way into the city where I had a reservation at an albergue. Being unable to figure out the metro or find someone who spoke English, I caught a taxi at the airport. The driver asked me what I was doing in Porto, and I told him about the Camino de Santiago, which he surprisingly knew nothing about. He asked if I was meeting up with a group, and I told him I was alone.

"You're crazy, man," he said, with a smile, as he glanced in the rearview mirror at me.

"Maybe a little bit."

I knew the Portuguese Way was not as popular as the French Way, but the lack of pilgrims around Porto still surprised me. After being dropped off in the center of the city and doing some sightseeing, I checked into the upscale albergue with automatic sliding doors at the entrance and waited for the

185

staff to finish cleaning for the evening. I met a group of four German pilgrims who arrived just after me, and they explained how they all met on the French Way three years before. After meeting Beth, Alma, and Regina on my first day on the trail last year, I envisioned finding a new group to walk with, but I was surprised when they explained they were taking a train tomorrow to bypass the first several miles through the city, something unheard of on the French Way.

Unlike their route, I would hike the Coastal Route of the Portuguese Way, which differed from the main route before rejoining one hundred fifteen miles away in the city of Redondela. From there I would walk another fifty miles to Santiago. This year, my Camino would not end in Santiago. I planned to continue another one hundred twenty-five miles on the loop to Finisterre and Muxia on the west coast, and back to Santiago. From there I would connect with a series of trails known as the Camino Ingles to the towns of Ferrol and A Coruna along the northern coast of Spain, and back to Santiago, adding an additional one hundred ninety-five miles. If I stuck to this plan, this walk would be a total of four hundred eighty-five miles, slightly less than the year before. My return flight was already booked for August 28 from Santiago.

Leaving the albergue on the morning of July 9, I walked through the dark cobblestone streets of Porto. I did not see any trail markers as I followed the river that would lead me to the coast. I knew the Portuguese Camino would not be as well marked as last year's route. This was one of the reasons I chose the Coastal Route. As long as the ocean was on my left I would not be lost.

I did not see another pilgrim through the entire morning darkness. Though I enjoyed the silence of being alone, something about this morning did not feel like being on the Camino. I felt like I was beginning an adventure truly on my own. As the city began to wake up, cars and buses flooded the road and people made their way down the streets, I felt out of place with my big backpack. Maybe this was what a true Camino was supposed to feel like.

My walk for the first day was fifteen miles to a campground near the town of Angeiras, where I had a one-room hut reserved for the night. I did not see another pilgrim on the trail until a group passed me a few miles from my destination. They all passed by without uttering more than hello. Clearly there would be no one on this trip who would compare to the group I was with at the beginning of my last Camino. The heat this morning was over one hundred degrees and had me dripping with sweat, but the crowded touristy beaches had a few quiet places to rest and cool off. I powered through the day as quickly as I could.

Upon arriving at the campground, I was completely exhausted from the heat and lay down in my air-conditioned hut. I noticed several pilgrims scattered among the dozen huts but did not engage any of them. Something about this Camino did not feel right, and I could not figure out why.

When I woke up on the morning of July 10, I realized today was my twenty-fifth birthday, but nothing about the day would be a celebration. Though I only had nine miles to walk, the humidity was so thick that each breath took immense effort and the temperature soared even higher than the day before. As I walked along boardwalks and coastal roads, my legs felt heavy, I was continuously out of breath, and my heart palpitated and jumped in and out of tempo. The strange sensations scared me, and I stopped for numerous breaks where I guzzled water and tried to calm my body. Maybe muscular dystrophy was finally catching up with me. Could the nine months since my last Camino have caused my body to change enough to make me no longer capable of walking long distances? I felt miserable and defeated when I reached my albergue in Povoa de Varzim. There were a handful of pilgrims there who did not speak English and kept to themselves. I walked to a restaurant and ordered a hamburger and a beer to celebrate my birthday.

My Own Pace

For three more days I trudged along the coast through the heat, doing ten-mile days without making any acquaintances except several bed bugs that left bites all over my body. Like déjà vu, the misery of my first Camino came back to me as bites multiplied each day. "Why am I doing this again?" I would say to myself each time I stopped to itch. Whenever the trail ventured inland, I regularly became disoriented as yellow arrows vanished, and I had to make my own route wandering through villages. Though the French Way had its fair share of missing markers, the Coastal Portuguese Camino was a completely different experience. I enjoyed the wildness, alone time, and breathtaking views of the Atlantic coast, but the more I was alone and lost, the more I thought of my friends and family, last year's Camino, and places like Wyoming where other adventures in my early twenties were centered around. Maybe the Camino experience could not be truly repeated. I kept asking myself why I returned. Did I have such a fun time that I wanted to repeat it? I was not sure anymore.

On the morning of July 14, on what was to be another long day, I had a sort of epiphany: I did not have to do this anymore. Though I was not going to quit my Camino, I knew there was no reason to walk the Camino Ingles after Finisterre and Muxia. By shaving off hundreds of miles, I could stop walking ten miles a day and instead do five mile days and put myself through less misery. As I wandered through the village of Carreço, which was initially only going to be my lunch stop, I saw a stone courtyard with a sign advertising Albergue Casa do Sardão next to an open wooden gate. Beyond the entrance was a large gazebo with overhanging vines and an old stone building surrounded by gardens of flowers and assorted vegetables. Without any hesitation, I knew this was where I would spend the night. As I walked inside, the dim overhead lights made it feel like I had gone underground. On the stone walls were various Camino themed knick-knacks, artwork, surfboards, and Buddhist prayer flags.

Journey's End

I was met at a front desk by a jittery, bald man dressed in plain, dark clothes, which did not seem to accurately reflect the eccentric bohemian vibe of the place. Nevertheless, the man was friendly and talkative and offered me a beer before showing me to the dorm room where I was given a bottom bunk. After a shower and a nap, I expected an uneventful evening but was awoken a few minutes later by a pair of familiar accents speaking English, something I had yet to encounter on this Camino. I jumped up and saw a couple in their early sixties. The man had long curly blond hair, and the woman had long flowing grey hair. After they put their things on their beds I greeted them.

The woman asked me where I was from, and she introduced herself and her husband as Donna and Scott from Ontario, Canada. They began their Camino in Lisbon several weeks before me and were walking with a man named Marcus from Puerto Rico they had met while walking the French Way two years earlier. Scott was a teacher and Donna worked in a school district, so they both had summers off to travel. When they walked the French Way the past two summers, they were forced to take buses through several sections due to injuries. Their goal on the Portuguese Camino was to walk the entire route. For the next week they planned to take short days to rest their bodies before the final push to Santiago, so I knew I would see them frequently in the coming days.

As they organized their gear, I went back to my nap and rested until dinner. Later in the afternoon I met their friend Marcus. He was in his mid-seventies, with a partially bald head and wearing glasses. Marcus turned out to be more American than I had expected. He was born in Paterson, New Jersey, grew up in Brooklyn, lived most of his adult life in Chicago, but had been living in Puerto Rico taking care of his mother for the past twenty years. Marcus was in severe pain and was having trouble with his knees. He had already taken several buses and trains throughout his journey. Today had been a test to see if he was feeling any better, but judging by how much trouble he had walking to the bathroom, it was obvious the test failed. By the sound of his voice, I could tell he knew his Camino was coming to an end.

I went to the kitchen later that evening to eat my dinner and found Donna sitting at the table writing in a journal. As we began sharing our stories from the Camino, I told her about how muscular dystrophy affects my journey and my desire to travel as much as I could before my condition progressed.

"Well, you have found a way to have time, money, and energy all at once," Donna said.

"Yeah, I guess I have," I said.

"Have you heard that expression before?" Donna asked, and went on to explain, "For the average person they are always missing one of those three things in life. When you are young you have time, energy, and no money, when you are middle-aged you have energy, money, and no time, and when you are old you have time, money, and no energy."

I laughed and said, "I guess you're right. At my age, usually only people who work at schools can have huge adventures three months out of every year."

"Hold on to it. Someone like you needs it more than anyone else."

The rest of the evening was relaxing, and we all sat in the lounge and drank beer. The albergue host played the movie *The Art of Flight*, a documentary about American snowboarders. As I watched the beautiful scenery of mountains in Colorado and Wyoming, I began to miss the American West. I knew if I had my summer off next year, I would make it a priority to return there. My time spent in Wyoming was where my spirit of adventure started, and I had been away from my roots for too long.

The next morning I began my new schedule. I walked six miles to the town of Ancora. By chance, I ended up in the same albergue as Donna, Scott, and Marcus. Marcus was in

Journey's End

the bed next to mine, so we talked for several hours about how miserable he was that his injuries had robbed him of what was to be his third and final Camino. He decided to take a train to Santiago tomorrow and fly home. Despite Marcus's sad story, I had my own problems to deal with. Tomorrow I was to make the crossing into Spain over the Minho River, but the ferry I planned to take was not running. Donna, Scott, and I made frantic plans to figure out how to cross the river. The nearest bridge was a day's walk out of the way and would add several days to our itineraries that would screw up all our schedules. Earlier that day I had booked my albergues all the way to Santiago, so tomorrow I had to be in the town of A Guarda on the Spanish side of the river, or all my reservations thereafter would be off by a day. Scott managed to talk to a few locals and found the telephone number of a fisherman named Tomás in the town of Caminha, who would supposedly ferry us across.

The next morning I woke up around 4:00 and walked the six miles to Caminha to be at the river to call Tomás before he began his day. Standing on the rocky shore of the river, with the Spanish coast slightly obscured in fog, I called the number and talked to an old man who gave me an address on the other side of town and told me to meet him there in fifteen minutes. When I arrived at the location, a man in his late seventies with a mangy-looking beard stepped out of a small dented car and directed me to put my pack in the trunk. With a bit of apprehension I got in the passenger seat. He drove in silence to a dock where another man stood by a motorized row boat. This man would take me across the river. My pack was loaded into the boat, and I found a seat among an assortment of fishing poles and equipment. The engine started with one pull of the rope and a puff of smoke, and we were on our way toward Spain. As we made our way across, the man said something in Portuguese.

"I don't speak Portuguese," I said.

He held up an ink stamp, and I knew he was asking if I needed a stamp in my credential book. I agreed, and he gave me a stamp just as our five minute boat ride came to an end.

"Welcome to Spain," he said, as he lifted my pack and dropped it in the sand.

"Thanks," I said, as I hopped out of the boat, shook his hand, and handed him five euros.

The man pointed toward the direction I needed to walk and said, "Bom Caminho," and turned the boat back to Portugal.

Taking my first steps in Spain since my last time there nine months before felt like returning home after being away for a long time. The four mile walk along the coast to A Guarda was relatively easy along boardwalk and paved road. Within the first few minutes I passed a woman walking down the road and greeted her with an enthusiastic, "Buenos días!"

Knowing only a few Spanish words, I felt completely fluent after not being able to utter a word of Portuguese. The woman smiled and said, "Buen Camino."

I passed a small farm with several black mountain boars behind a fenced-in area, and I recalled how I survived my last time in Spain on bocadillo jamón. Seeing my food in living form made me surprisingly hungry, and I knew the first thing I needed to do in Spain. I came across an open café on the outskirts of A Guarda and ordered a bocadillo jamón and a cold beer before 10:00. I survived my trek through Portugal; this was an occasion to celebrate.

Donna and Scott, who were able to find another fisherman to take them across the river, met me at the municipal albergue in A Guarda later that afternoon, and we found a pizza restaurant in town for dinner. For the next four days, we all continued at our slow pace and were able to stay at the same albergue, making them the longest trail friends I had made on both Caminos, at seven days in a row before separating.

The last day with them turned out to be one of my most difficult days on the Portuguese Camino. The night before, while having dinner together in Vigo, Scott said, "I'm looking forward to the walk to Redondela tomorrow. Our guidebook says it will be a flat walk through an enchanted shaded forest." After several days of quite hilly terrain, I was glad to hear the word "flat" in any trail description.

There was a gradual climb and a split in the trail as I first made my way out of Vigo. Trail markers pointed both ways, but the markers going up the hill had brighter paint, so I assumed that was the way. The trail led to an amazing view of Vigo with a backdrop of the bright blue ocean. This was to be my last view of the coast as the Coastal Route would soon connect with the Inland Route. My guidebook noted several viewpoints, so I thought I was on the correct trail. The day was turning hot, and the trail continued to get steeper. I kept hoping it would flatten out after this hill. Knowing a "flat enchanted shaded forest" lay ahead motivated me to keep moving. Eventually the trail led onto a busy road lined with sticker bushes. My legs slowly got scraped raw, and the road continued heading uphill. A tear rolled down my cheek as I strained to keep walking.

"Ugh! I want to go home!" I yelled out. After a few more minutes, I made it to a flat area where I could take a rest.

Looking back down the road I yelled out, "There's nothing flat, enchanted, shaded, or forested about this!"

I double checked my guidebook; it noted a few ups and downs but generally the land stayed level. I was sure I had taken the right road back at the split. I trudged on, hoping all this uphill would lead somewhere. On another steep section I slipped and scraped the palms of my hands on the hot blacktop. At the top of the hill, I came to another split where arrows pointed in two different directions. One way went uphill and one way went downhill. I chose downhill, hoping that it would lead to the forest.

The downhill route led to a dirt trail, and there I discovered a new set of trail markers. This was the trail I needed to be on.

Before long, it led into a cool shaded forest and passed a small waterfall. "Now this is enchanting," I thought, as I stopped to rest for a few minutes.

The remainder of my ten-mile day was rather relaxing, but my feet were in a great deal of pain after walking uphill on the unnecessary detour. At the albergue in Redondela when I reconnected with Donna and Scott, they explained how they continued farther up the hill at the second split. Their way was even steeper and continued for several additional miles before leading into Redondela from a different direction.

Scott chuckled in an annoyed tone and said, "I feel like taking a taxi back up there and spray painting an 'X' on all those arrows pointing uphill."

"I was so excited this morning for an easy walk that it completely pissed me off that we walked up that hill," Donna said.

"Me too. It felt like everything I set my hopes on today crumbled before me," I said.

"It's easy to be happy when you plan for happy things. When those happy plans turn sour, we face a potentially dark place in our minds. But today made me realize I never want to see that part of my mind again. Sometimes we need a dark place to see the light," Donna said.

"That just about sums up my day," I laughed.

I thought a lot about what Donna said and realized this journey had been a less enlightening experience than last year. I returned to the Camino with the intention of recreating the insights I learned before, but instead found something different. The Portuguese Camino taught me that discoveries cannot be planned, they simply happen.

My night in Redondela was the last with Donna and Scott, but there I met a man in his early fifties named Lee from Florida. He was the first American I encountered on this Camino. Marcus, who I met several days before, was technically an American, but he identified as Puerto Rican.

Journey's End

This lack of Americans on the Portuguese Camino added to the feelings of remoteness I felt on this journey. The next day I walked to the town of Arcade. I arrived at the albergue before 10:00 a.m. and sat at a table outside and waited for Donna and Scott to pass by to say goodbye. Around noon they arrived with Lee and stopped to join me for lunch. For the next seven days, I continued on alone, not meeting a single native English speaker despite the population of the Camino increasing after I rejoined the main route.

On July 28, I stopped at the town of O Milladoiro, five miles short of Santiago. At the albergue I met two American girls who were life-long friends from Georgia who recently graduated from college. For dinner we went to a grocery store and bought vegetables and the makings for sandwiches. Two other pilgrims joined us, a Portuguese guy and an Italian girl who were both around my age. After dinner we played card games and drank wine to celebrate our near completion of the Camino. The next day we all agreed to meet in Santiago for another celebration. All of their walks would end in Santiago, but I would be continuing on.

Arriving in Santiago the next morning, twenty-one days after leaving Porto, lacked the triumphant feeling I had the year before. This was not the end of my journey because my sights were set on the coast. Some claim Finisterre is the true end and others claim Muxia is the end. I planned to walk to both towns, but after Muxia I would walk back to Santiago, so ultimately Santiago would be the final end.

After receiving my Compostela certificate in Santiago on July 29, the man behind the counter offered me a ticket for a free meal at a fancy hotel called the Parador. Initially I was confused by his generosity, but I learned that every day ten pilgrims were chosen for the meal as they collected their Compostelas. After checking into the same albergue and the same bed as the year before, I made my way to the Parador. Inside this large and luxurious stone building, I was seated in a small back room at a long table with settings for ten people. Lunch was chicken soup and roast pork that was tender and juicy with a crispy skin and mouth-watering seasonings, and chocolate flan for dessert. Other pilgrims at the table varied not only in age and nationality but in their Camino routes. From the Portuguese to the French Way, to the De Norte, Via de la Plata, Ingles, and Primitivo, everyone came from different locations throughout the Iberian Peninsula to reach Santiago. I suspected this diversity was most likely intentional and part of the selection process for this lunch.

Leaving Santiago on July 31 after a rest day, I felt as if I was continuing the journey from last October. For nine days I walked a total of fifty-four miles, in roughly five-mile-day segments. The distance could have been completed in three days, but I was done pushing my body to its limits. The walk to Finisterre was much quieter than the Portuguese Camino, and half of the nights I was the only pilgrim at the albergues. Thirty-one days and two hundred thirty miles after leaving Porto, on the morning of August 8, before sunrise, I stood on a narrow peninsula, surrounded by rocks and the crashing waves of the Atlantic Ocean. A feeling of complete peace came over me as I realized this was the most breathtaking scenery I had ever seen. I understood why the ancient humans who settled this land thought this was the end of the world. Looking out across the endless expanse of water, I too felt as if the world ended here.

"I want to go home," I said to myself as I began to softly shed several tears.

The thought of walking over seventy more miles to Muxia and back to Santiago seemed unnecessary. My demons were conquered, and my inner strength had already been found. This was the feeling that eluded me at the end of my last Camino: a feeling that I had reached the end, a feeling that there was nothing more to prove, and now I was there. True strength is about standing at the edge of something bigger than yourself and knowing that nothing but your own inner grit brought you there.

My flight home was not until August 28, so later that evening I changed my return date to August 11. I wanted to be home more than anything else. When I stood at the edge of the Cape of Finisterre, I thought about everything that led me here, and how it all started back in Wyoming, where my spirit of adventure was born. The two weeks I gained from not staying in Spain would be used to return to my roots.

Three days after returning home, I jumped in a car with my friend Mike and hit the road. In just over a day, we drove halfway across the United States to Wyoming. The last time I was in Wyoming was 2014, but time did not seem to pass. This was the only place away from New Jersey that felt like a home to me.

After waking up at my uncle Jeb's the next morning, Mike and I drove to the ranch where I worked in 2013. One of the managers let us walk around and tour the ranch, but everything seemed strange and foreign. Nothing had changed yet everything had changed. This place had such an impact on my life that I always thought seeing it again would be fulfilling, but instead I felt empty. Besides the managers, all of the staff I knew were gone. Like the Camino, I already took away everything I needed from this place. I was glad to see it again, but there was no reason to ever return.

After seeing the ranch, Jeb drove us up into the mountains near Encampment to see the old cabin where he used to live. We drove the washed-out roads as far as we could, then hiked the rest of the way. Since I was last here four years ago, the cabin was in worse shape than I remembered. Overgrown trees, bushes, sage brush, and animals were taking back the land. The door was missing, the roof was beginning to collapse, and the walls had many holes where light poured through. When I was young and heard stories of Jeb's wandering years and living in the mountains, I dreamed of one day living in this cabin and recreating the vision of Wyoming I romanticized in my mind. That dream was now gone.

While we were at the cabin, Uncle Jeb said, "I didn't know what I was looking for during my wandering years, but when I saw this place I knew I found it."

Part of me always knew this was what the cabin represented, but now it was clear. This was Jeb's place and no one else's. The cabin became a metaphor about undiscovered dreams. My "cabin" was out there somewhere, but I just had not found it yet. Wyoming was still a location I loved more than most places, but something about its meaning to me died that day. Now I realized my dreams were bigger than this place. I needed to return here after my second Camino to understand this. Insights come from new places and new experiences.

From where we stood, surrounded by rolling mountains covered in sagebrush and dry grasses, Medicine Bow Peak was visible on the distant horizon and capped with snow. I thought back to when I picked up my rock on the summit, and then about when I left it at Cruz de Ferro. Those memories seemed like a lifetime ago, but today's date was August 18, 2018, a year to the day since I began walking the Camino in St-Jean. In that year I had trekked seven hundred thirty miles around the Iberian Peninsula, only to return to Wyoming. This adventure had come to its final end, but the real journey had just begun. There were places in the world I needed to discover and people I needed to meet.

Tom's words still resonate in my mind, when he said, "There is no such thing as slow on the Camino; there is only your own pace. We all have our own difficulties, and we all deal with them in our own ways." Walking at my own pace became a basis for understanding strength, which I no longer viewed as a linear measurement but rather a reflection of my will to persevere. The defects in our DNA, in some cases, may define what we are physically, but they do not need to define who we are. No matter how we find ourselves in this world, we cannot deny the beauty of life that we all have the choice to discover.

AFTERWORD
BY JEB STEWARD

First, I want to thank you for reading Bryan's story, and I hope it has enriched your life as much as being a part of Bryan's life has enriched my life. Bryan was very generous to share his story with the world . . . a special gift. I hope his gift to you is like a song you will listen to over and over again. Giving and receiving, the symbiotic relationship that was revealed to Bryan throughout his journey.

I remember the day Bryan and I climbed to the top of Medicine Bow Peak very well. Two people having an adventure on a mountain, living in the moment. It was a Good Day! Perhaps, in hindsight though, in that moment I was not aware of the magnitude of this event on Bryan's life. Sometimes we are not fully aware of these life changing events until later, much later. I am left wondering if having that knowledge then would have made the day more meaningful for me or not. We can only wonder about these things, but I am sure this is how it is supposed to be. We are better to live in the moment, and instead, celebrate these times when we are old.

This is not just another story about someone doing great things in the face of adversity or being able to just play the hand life has dealt, this is the story of someone truly living their life. This book may not be easy reading for those who think life is fair and if you screw something up you will get a second chance. Hopefully, this story will be meaningful to

Afterword

those who have never done something larger than themselves, and perhaps this book can be an inspiration to finally find the courage to go do it. But you don't get courage just from reading a book.

Bryan's story is about grit. It's about showing a little try and then giving it some more. It's about falling down and getting back up again, and again, and again . . . literally. You either have grit or you don't. This story is also about how, somewhere along the road, life happens! This is the story of that journey as we strive and struggle to understand ourselves from someone who must also struggle with physical barriers that most people do not even understand. Bryan demonstrates that the journey is more important than the destination, or maybe, the journey is the destination.

Some of us are doomed not to know what we are looking for until we find it because we are wanderers. People have always been going to the desert, climbing mountains, or trying to find solitude in order to clear their mind and hear their inner voice, driven by the knowledge that a truly meaningful life requires deep contemplation.

Bryan's story can be a story for the Everyman, the story about how anyone can find strength when facing the unknown and sensing your insignificance while standing on the edge of the abyss with compassion, confidence, and courage.

Enjoy the rest of your Journey, my friend Bryan. I see more great things in your future.

ACKNOWLEDGMENTS

I want to thank the countless pilgrims who offered their help and words of encouragement throughout my journey. I am forever in your debt. I also want to thank my former boss, Roseann, for allowing me the time off from work to have this journey, and Roger Brucker for schooling me in the art of writing.

Thank you to my parents, for instilling a sense of wonder in me, and for putting up with me during my traveling years, which came with sleepless nights wondering where in the world I was.

Thank you to my friends and family who walked with me while I trained for the Camino and for reading over many portions of this book as I edited over the past four years.

And to my fiancée, Madeline, for being my most honest editor, and for all your love and understanding as I spent countless hours finishing this project. This book would never have been finished if it were not for you.

ABOUT THE AUTHOR

After graduating from The College of New Jersey in 2016, with a degree in Communications, author Bryan Steward spent several years traveling and working odd jobs before settling down in his home state of New Jersey. He still enjoys going for walks, writing, and traveling whenever he gets the chance.

He reflects on his Camino experience often and uses the lessons of the journey to overcome new obstacles he continues to face. Stay tuned for upcoming works on his travels and reflections on living with a neuromuscular disease.

If you have any questions, feedback, or are interested in having Bryan as a guest speaker, he can be contacted at: myownpace.bryan.steward@gmail.com

TOP: Day 1 in St-Jean-Pied-de-Port
BOTTOM: Monuments at the summit of Alto de Perdón

TOP: At Cruz de Ferro
BOTTOM: Crossing the Pyrenees Mountains

TOP: Passing through Viana
BOTTOM: Trekking across the mountains of Galicia

TOP: At the End Of The World in Finisterre
BOTTOM: In front of the Cathedral in Santiago de Compostela

Printed in Great Britain
by Amazon

78172791R00128